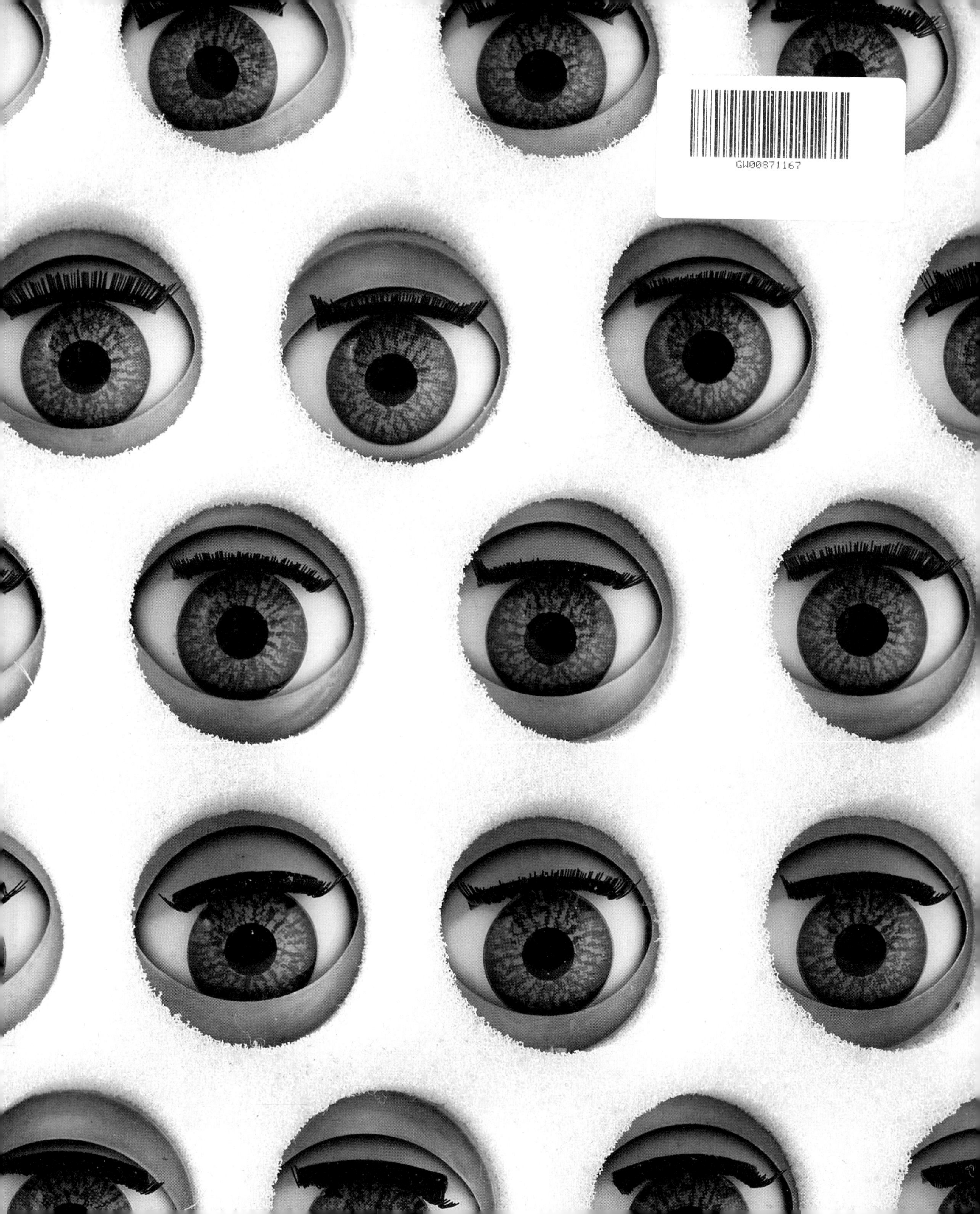

Shoes for the Moscow Circus

For FGF and WFK

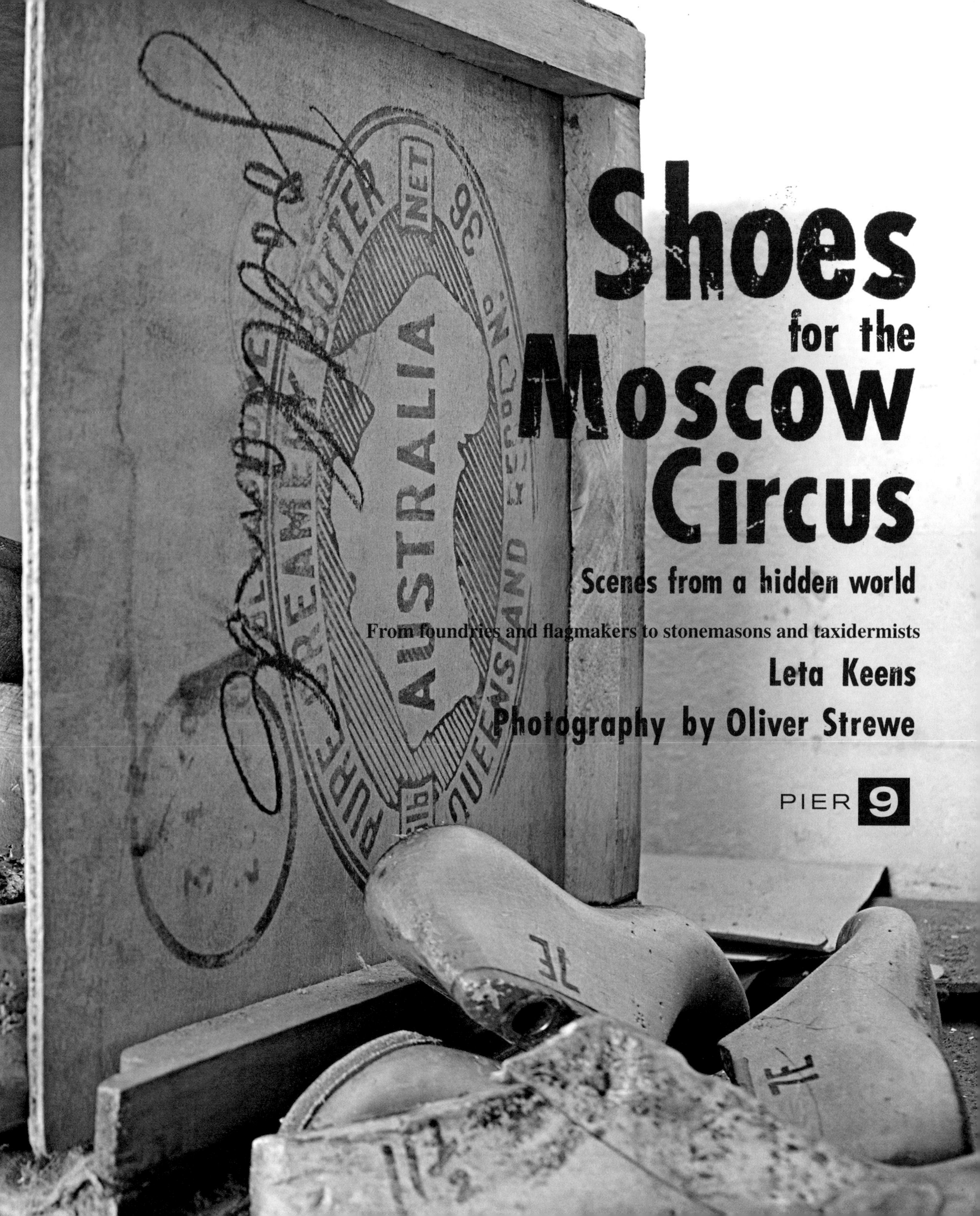

Shoes for the Moscow Circus

Scenes from a hidden world

From foundries and flagmakers to stonemasons and taxidermists

Leta Keens

Photography by Oliver Strewe

PIER 9

BOX 18
SILVER CUPS:
S.C. SERIES
BOX 14 TOP
BOX 26
JEWISH MINORA.
WEDDING CAKE VASE.
HALF TABERNACLE BALLS.
MASS BELL STEMS.
VOTIVE CANDLE SOCKETS - SARKS.
CARIS - LADLES + SPOONS.
CHALICE
305} 905} BASES+BOWLS
35} 295} ALL SIZES
SANCTUARY LAMPS:
533 (3 SIZES).
543.
547.
BOX 35
MONSTRANCES:
STANDARD BOXES.
LUNETTE
BOX 36
MONSTRANCES:
GOLD CUPS
BOX 11 TOP

Years ago I visited a terrazzo factory in one of Sydney's inner-city industrial suburbs. As I remember it, when it was being set up in the Twenties, hardly anyone in Australia knew how to make terrazzo. Expert workers were brought in from Italy. Women from the same area were brought here too; the idea was that they would marry the men. That happened, more or less, and a whole community developed. In the Eighties, terrazzo was all the rage. So, too, was having a co-ordinated look in the house. You could go down to this factory with a wallpaper or fabric swatch, and have your terrazzo flooring specially made to match. You could also have all sorts of things put into the terrazzo – chips of glass as well as different stones. The factory had developed their terrazzo-making techniques to such a level that they were taking in orders from Italy.

The factory isn't there anymore, but occasionally I've thought about the workers who had been there for more than half a century, the piles of sample terrazzo in Eighties greys, dusty pinks and sage greens, the room of rusty 44-gallon drums filled with intensely coloured powdered pigments. I've also thought about a terracotta factory I visited at the same time, which made chimney pots, tiles and planters in a massive corrugated iron building with a sawtooth roof. In the middle of the factory was a salt-glazing kiln, the inside of which was iced up with a crust of brilliant blue glaze.

Factories and workshops are disappearing from Australian cities and towns for a number of reasons. Land in the inner-city, for a start, is more valuable for housing than other things – and once a few blocks of apartments go up in an area, the last thing the new residents want is a factory nearby, even if it has been there for half a century.

A lot of industry, admittedly, is filthy – factories have disappeared as pollution laws have tightened. And dangerous, too – occupational health and safety has stopped many practices. Some places the photographer and I visited almost certainly would not be allowed to start up in their present locations if they applied to do so today.

At the same time, consumers have become obsessively acquisitive, wanting more of everything, instantly and cheaper – and if that means buying goods made offshore at wages far lower than any Australian worker would ever be paid or, conveniently, at the local supermarket or chain store, then that's the way it has to be.

Shoes for the Moscow Circus

While all this has been happening, teenagers have been staying on at school longer. And somewhere along the way, apprenticeships have become scarcer and it has become increasingly difficult, in some areas, to find skilled labour.

When I started writing this book, I had a feeling I was going to be documenting businesses that were on the way out. That thought was taken to extremes when one of the first places I contacted, a chaff merchant near Wagga Wagga, NSW, and my lead for haystack builders, told me I was too late, they'd stopped making them about a year earlier as it was too hard to find workers and, anyway, the haystacks were so high they'd need to put scaffolding around them to meet current occupational health and safety requirements. I almost gave up at that point. Quite by chance it turned out that Oliver Strewe had photographed haystack making in the area about 25 years ago, and it's his old shots we're using in the last chapter, as a poignant reminder of what can disappear.

Some of the places we visited did seem endangered, but I discovered not all is completely lost in the world of Australian trades and industries. A number of the businesses we came across have been working quietly and steadily for years, with enough work to keep them going, and customers both here and overseas. Some are expanding, and making positive steps, including paying decent wages and providing in-house training, to encourage young people into the area.

I could have covered any number of different trades and industries – for purely personal reasons, I decided to concentrate mainly on those that produce usable items, and are not directly involved with food, fashion or furniture, which, I feel, do get some attention elsewhere.

While I was working on the book, the most common response I had from friends, colleagues and anyone else interested was amazement that certain products were made in this country. *Shoes for the Moscow Circus* aims to draw attention to one aspect of the Australian working life that, I believe, is either undervalued or, far too often, ignored.

Taxidermy

South Pacific Taxidermy is next door to the Suraj Group Indian grocery warehouse in a Melbourne trade park. No one's at the taxidermy studio when we arrive, but we know we're at the right place. A red Hyundai hatchback is in the car park – the head of a mountain goat and a few horns are in the back; something's lying under a grey blanket. All we can smell is cumin and coriander from the Suraj Group, which has as its slogan 'Shine Above the Rest'. The owner's sweeping the floor. We check out his shop, look at his collection of Bollywood movies, buy some cardamom, and talk about rice.

'You must see some strange sights coming and going from next door,' we say.

'Ah yes, I feed the birdy, he make the birdy,' he says. 'But he's a very good neighbour, good friend of mine, very nice man, honest man.'

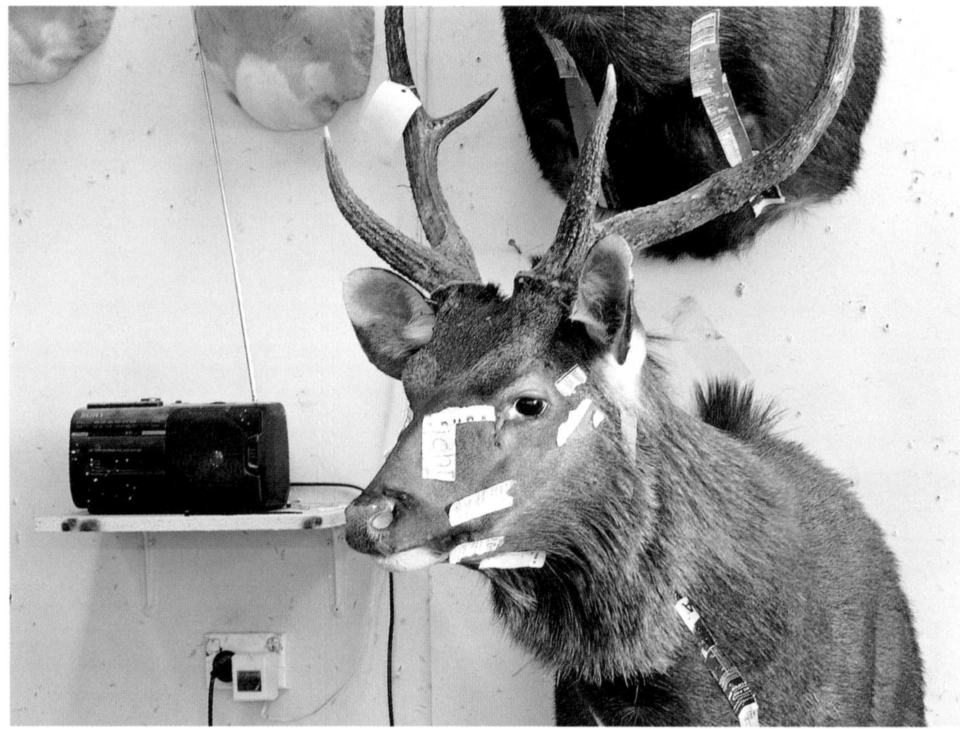

We look through the windows of South Pacific Taxidermy, the largest commercial taxidermy business in Australia, and a mob of kangaroos is next to a crocodile, a sulphur-crested cockatoo is beside a goat, a gazelle by a dingo. Apart from the distinct lack of pairs, this could be a chaotic, light industrial version of Noah's Ark.

Gary Pegg, wearing jeans, a T-shirt and a baseball cap, arrives after a few minutes and opens up. Near the front of the workshop a wallaby is holding a broom. Not the only spot for the broom, says Gary Pegg. 'It just ends up with whatever has paws.' Pegboards of tools at the back of workbenches look like those in the average garden shed – pliers, saws, hammers – nothing unusual. And knives from a professional kitchen, needles from a sewing basket.

The hangar-like workspace and adjoining room (which also contains a couple of mattresses – a strange place to stay the night) is packed with birds and animals at various stages of the taxidermy process, the finished ones looking alert, as if a moment in their lives has been captured. For those partway through the process, it's slightly more confronting: an owl is bound with knitting wool for a few days to keep its wings in place; the body of a kangaroo is littered with scraps of waxed cardboard from a Rev milk carton, stuck down with small rows of pins outlining delicate threads of veins, features that need time to form. Waxed card is used as it doesn't stick to the fur, says Gary Pegg.

Some creatures, inelegantly, and not on public view, have their heads wrapped in bubble wrap. Still the only smells that waft through the space are the Indian spices from next door, and it's only after I've left South Pacific Taxidermy that I realise I didn't touch on anything gruesome with Gary Pegg. It didn't enter my mind while I was there.

Gary Pegg's unprepossessing office, lined in sheets of timber veneer, has birds on every shelf. A bird of paradise with exuberant plumage, parrots, galahs, tiny birds, antique birds under glass, a bird in a cardboard grocery box. A cabinet of skulls. Books about birds. The screensaver on his computer has rolling pictures of birds, and sheep from North America and an African antelope – creatures he has worked on over the years. Certificates on the wall have, among others, Gary Pegg as best in the world for birds in 1999 with his black cockatoo, an overall winner the same year for four of his pieces, including a platypus and a yellow-bibbed lory. 'I always keep them very simple,' he says, to explain his success. 'Sometimes people have this idea they have to make the whole thing extravagant or with an action pose. I just do a more natural pose, like it's out in the wild.'

Gary Pegg's first taxidermy experiment, as a 16 year old, was a duck. 'A game bird my brother had shot, and it looked OK – I still have visions of it, I remember its legs were too far back but otherwise it was fairly good for a first attempt, I thought.' He bought a couple of books on taxidermy from a Melbourne bookshop and subscribed to a correspondence course run by a man in Sydney. 'Very basic, very introductory but it got you started and interested.'

He loved birds, and collected dead ones, which would have been thrown away otherwise, from breeders. Even now, apart from trophies collected by hunters, most of his specimens come, dead mainly of natural causes, from zoos and fauna parks.

14

A lot of people, says Gary Pegg, 'think because you're a taxidermist you run out and kill wildlife, they don't understand that in zoos and fauna parks animals die of old age or of accidents or other causes. It's part of life – when you have live ones, you'll have dead ones. That's the way it is. But there's no reason whatsoever to kill any animals.'

There's an unexpected gentleness to him – he talks more about conservation, loss of habitat and his love for birds than I would have imagined. I'm not sure what I was expecting – my only contact with taxidermy is a savage-looking chicken that sits in my living room, the first attempt by another animal-loving teenager, who went on to become a racehorse trainer. Everyone, says Gary Pegg, starts with a chicken, rat, rabbit or duck. They're easy to get hold of and small and easy to handle.

'It's a total fascination, when you appreciate the beauty of something, that's what draws you to it. It intrigues you to see these animals, and a big pity to see them lost because there's no other way to have them preserved and appreciated. People take photographs, I suppose, which is the main way they have a memory of something. Taxidermy adds another dimension.' He can accept that some people may find that approach macabre.

When he left school and joined the Board of Works as a draftsman, taxidermy was a hobby for Gary Pegg. But in 1983, after he came back from the first world show in Atlanta, Georgia, he was offered a job with a taxidermist in Gippsland. 'I couldn't see any future in the Board of Works at the time. It was a monotonous sort of job, sitting at a drafting board. You could do a design over several weeks and it would suddenly be scrapped, gone, finished. It seemed such a waste of energy. I saw what I was doing at that stage as a taxidermist as you'd start with something and finish with something. You'd see things materialise, and they could remain in museums or collections for hundreds of years. Those birds hanging on the wall over there were done in 1850.' He points to a clutch of birds on a branch under a glass dome. 'Whoever did them, those birds are still here 150 years later. It's better than having a drawing torn up before you and thrown in the rubbish.'

I can't help saying the word 'stuffed' when I'm talking to Gary Pegg. It slips out three or four times, but, politely, he doesn't correct me. His animals are not stuffed. That's not how taxidermy is done these days. Animals used to be stuffed, often with

straw like a Guy Fawkes dummy, and that's why they looked overblown and unnatural. For the past 40 years, hard polyurethane foam forms in the basic shapes of the animals have been used to drape the skin over. Before that happens, the skin is cured or tanned – for birds that might take a few hours, for larger creatures a couple of days. Gary Pegg has dozens of different foam forms of the most common animals he deals with – grey kangaroos, red kangaroos, rock wallabies, feral goats, feral pigs, red deer, foxes. Many, in small, medium or large, are available for sale to other taxidermists (as are glass eyes for various animals – sitting like prize marbles in drawers in his office). There's a foam fruit bat hanging, a standing brushtail possum, a platypus swimming. Poses can be altered by sawing through the foam, rearranging the body parts, filling or smoothing over gaps and gluing it all back together.

Most birds don't have a standard form – Gary Pegg just sculpts each from a block of foam. And for the more unusual animals, he, or one of the two people who work with him, may need to use artists' plasticine over the skeleton to sculpt the body shape and then make a one-off fibreglass mould from which a form is taken. That was the case with a commission from the Hong Kong Jockey Club – River Verdon, a champion racehorse that had won the Hong Kong Cup twice, the Triple Crown twice, and had died of old age at a retirement park at Sunbury, near Melbourne airport. It was a very large horse, and no prefabricated body at South Pacific Taxidermy came close to it.

'Being a racehorse it was very particular in structure,' says Gary Pegg. 'When he died, he was out of his racing prime. Like a lot of us, he'd put on weight and looked nothing like he did in his youth, nice and slick and racy looking. I said to the owner, "You've got to understand he's 19 years old, we can't make the excess skin disappear."' He was told to do River Verdon, now at the Hong Kong Jockey Club, as he was 'when he passed away. His condition was good, it was just he was a bit fat and happy.' Gary Pegg made a dead horse for the most recent Ned Kelly movie. 'You put so much detail into it and it's on the screen for a second – it was a half-dark, stormy night and you see a dead horse lying on the ground and that's it. You think "That's movies."'

With animal welfare being high priority and computer animation being highly advanced, he gets a fair bit of work with commercials. 'If they can't use a trained animal in a particular shot, they'll see if we've got a mounted one, and then do adjustments on the computer.'

Other specimens of Gary Pegg's, mainly Australian natives, are in museums in Indonesia, China and Taiwan. One of the most unusual animals he has had to deal with was an echidna. 'What's fascinating is getting up close and having contact with the specimens to see their various features – things you wouldn't notice if you were looking at an animal in a pen. The claws on the echidna for digging termites out of the wood. And its quills, which float on the body with a membrane between, almost like a suit of armour.' Injuries from dead animals have been minimal. 'They haven't had their opportunity to get back at me. You might be working, and lift your head and thump it on something, that's about the extent of it.'

While animals that were once stuffed with straw now have their skins draped over a foam frame, other innovations have made their way into the taxidermy business. The same material used inside the toe pieces of shoes is used for the inserts of animal ears. Automotive paints and putties, and dental plasters, are now in the taxidermy studio. Kevlar thread, developed for the space industry, has been used for more than 20 years to sew up animals. 'It's nice and strong – and then for about the same length of time, superglue instead of thread for very fine, delicate work. We heard the medical industry started using that much later to close up incisions.'

Hair dye is also used at times. 'We were repairing a tiger skin and the new pieces were a lot brighter than the old ones so we had to tone them back. You go into the hairdressing supplies shop and ask for colours or bleaches and when they ask what you want them for, and you say "I'm working on a tiger", they sort of look at you a bit strange.'

Gary Pegg is happy to work on virtually any animal. The ones he likes working on least are family pets. 'It's such an emotional area. Sometimes the people may be acting on a reflex sort of thing than a real conscious decision. I try to talk them out of it, especially if there are kids involved – the best thing to do is for them to get a new one. I suppose because I see life and death, life and death, I deal with it.' And no one's pet, he says, is ordinary. 'It's never a standard dog, its tail bends a bit differently or its mouth used to drop in one corner, or its ear is a bit higher on one side – it's all those things you have to deal with. You have to get onto those little quirks to show the quirky individual it was.' And when the owner comes to pick it up, 'they come with its special basket and the cushion it sleeps with, the toy it would play with. You think maybe they need to let go, but that's human behaviour.'

When his own dog, a shih-tzu, died 'I must admit we got it cremated. That was eight years ago. We had a young child at the time, he had to be put down – the dog, that is. I put him in an urn and remember him that way. We've got him in a cupboard with his ball, and that's Spencer. We moved straight on and got another pet, a little female maltese cross, and on you go with life.'

On a shelf in the back room at South Pacific Taxidermy, surrounded by native wildlife and birds, is a lively looking fox terrier, pastel collar on, looking as if he's ready for a walk. 'I tried to talk the owners out of having him done, but they insisted.' But they were some of the ones who moved on – they never came back for him, never paid for him.

'He's been in a commercial with a Paris Hilton look-alike, has been hired out for a few things. He's paid his way, he's part of the furniture. I'm quite attached to him.'

Robes for Clergy

22

The only piece of advice Claire de Muth's father-in-law gave her and husband Dennis when they bought Church Stores from him in 1995 was not to ask prospective staff members about their religious beliefs. Dealing with clergy of all Christian denominations and occasionally doing handmade millinery work for the Great Synagogue, it's best, she says, not to be 'too one way or the other' on the religious front. 'All we look for in staff is that they have decent values.' It doesn't seem right to ask Claire de Muth if she's religious. She does say, though, that people tend to give her the wide berth at parties when they hear what kind of business she's in, worrying that she might try to convert them. You get the impression it's not a vocation – she started out in the wine business and ended up in reinsurance underwriting before dealing in the ecclesiastical. 'It's not something I ever dreamt I'd be doing.'

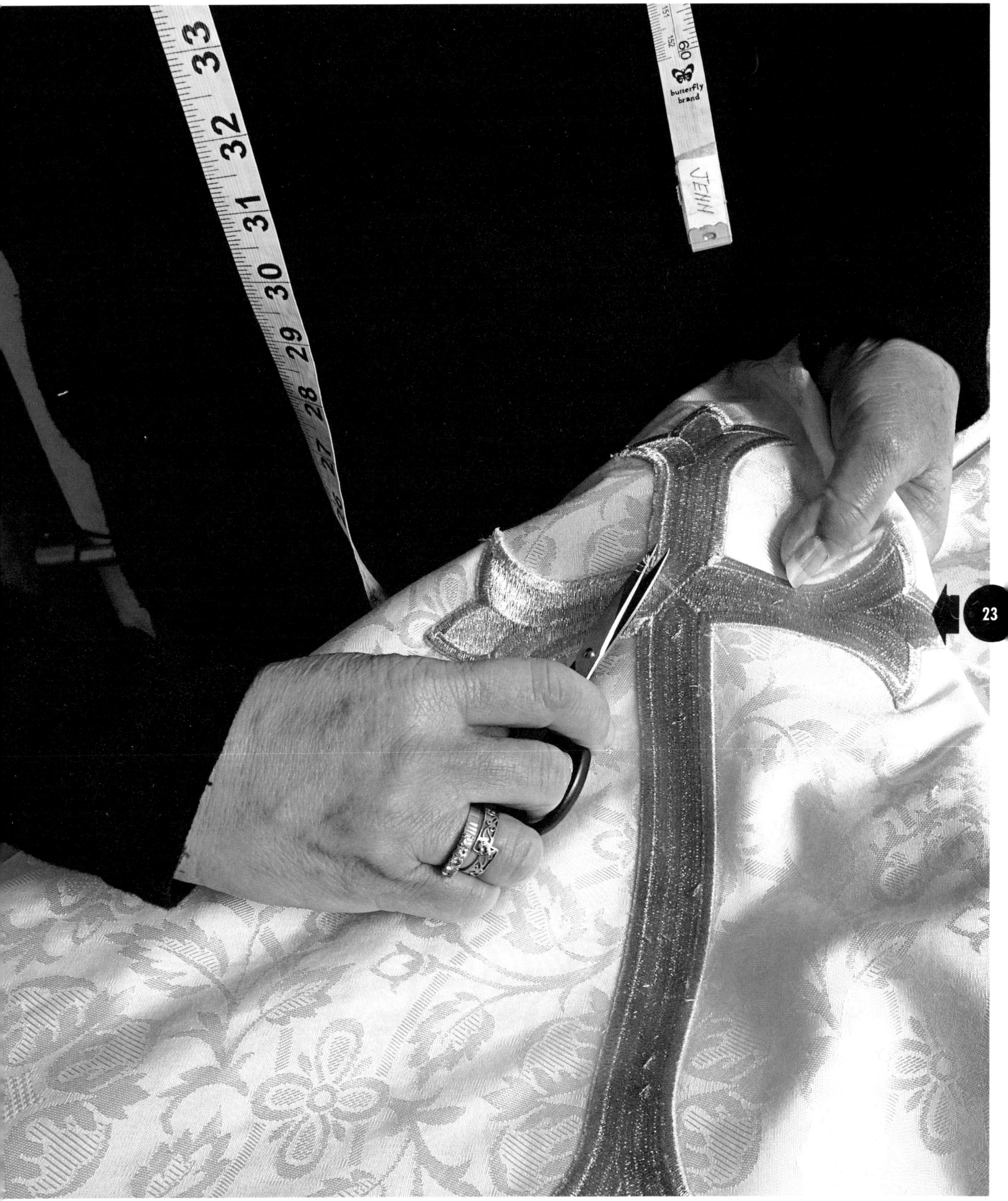
butterfly brand

That's the first surprise about Church Stores, a business that makes altar cloths, banners and other church accessories as well as surplices, albs and other religious wear, many of which are one-off pieces. 'We're very much a boutique organisation,' says Claire de Muth. It's hidden away in the Dymocks Building in the centre of Sydney, a building with an esoteric combination of tenants – from bridal shops and Celtic specialists to new age therapy practitioners and a traveller's medical centre.

The second surprise is that Church Stores had made some of the costumes for *Shout!*, the musical about rock-and-roll singer Johnny O'Keefe. Priests' robes, authentic to look at but quick to get out of. The company is also asked, from time to time, to make ecclesiastical costumes – historically and culturally accurate – for Opera Australia and the Sydney Theatre Company.

Actually, the first surprise of all about Church Stores is that they agreed to do an interview during Sydney World Youth Day, the Catholic celebrations that brought hundreds of thousands of visitors, and the Pope, to the city. 'Yes, we have been busy,' says Claire de Muth. 'Mainly in the lead-up, though, when a lot of parishes were refurbishing their churches. It's been more about the churches than anything – a lot of them are sponsoring pilgrims,' and presumably want to look their best. But then, 'we made a mitre last week for a bishop who wanted one in a hurry – I don't know if he forgot his, or whether it didn't survive the trip'. And adjustments have been made on various albs and stoles. 'People from Germany and Canada, for whatever reason, needed robes.'

Generally, the company's business is Australia-wide, but among its 2500 account customers, it does have clients in the Pacific. 'And with the internet, we're getting quite a few enquiries from the United States.' Although all dealings can happen over mail and email, with clients sending a sketch of what they want and Church Stores sending out fabric samples 'and to-ing and fro-ing until we settle on a project', says manager Helen Faulks, who worked as a TAFE fashion teacher for many years, 'it's far easier for us to work on a garment if we deal with the person face to face. It gives us an idea of intangible things we can't get from correspondence – things you can pick up in body language. You know immediately if you're on the right track – it's such an organic process, I don't try to analyse it.' Her main regret, she says, is that she doesn't get to see most of the garments in situ. 'Quite often, though, they send us photographs.'

Like her attitude towards employees, Claire de Muth has a similarly secular approach towards clients. The preacher could be Methodist, Uniting or Presbyterian – no one's asking questions or asking for identification. He or she may not even be a member of the clergy, but it's not advisable to go into Church Stores and ask for a pope's outfit for a fancy dress party. 'We have to tell them we don't keep such a thing on the shelf…the Pope does have his own tailors in Rome.'

It's best to keep quiet if you want any of their religious wear at all for fancy dress. 'If we know that's what it's for, we try to dissuade them,' says Helen Faulks. 'We're not being elitist, but our products have some reverence attached to them. It's not our place to question people's motives, but it's fortunate we're not streetfront. It's interesting that the type of thing we sell does attract some people who are less than dedicated in their outlook to what it's all about.'

The business started out as a bookshop in the St James crypt in King Street in 1904, and got its name, Church Stores, when it moved to the Queen Victoria Building in 1912 at a time when Penfold's Wines was in the basement and the municipal library was in a rambling space upstairs. Church Stores only stayed for three or four years, before it moved to Daking House, now a youth hostel, near Central Station. In the early Eighties it moved to the Dymocks Building, where it sells virtually everything

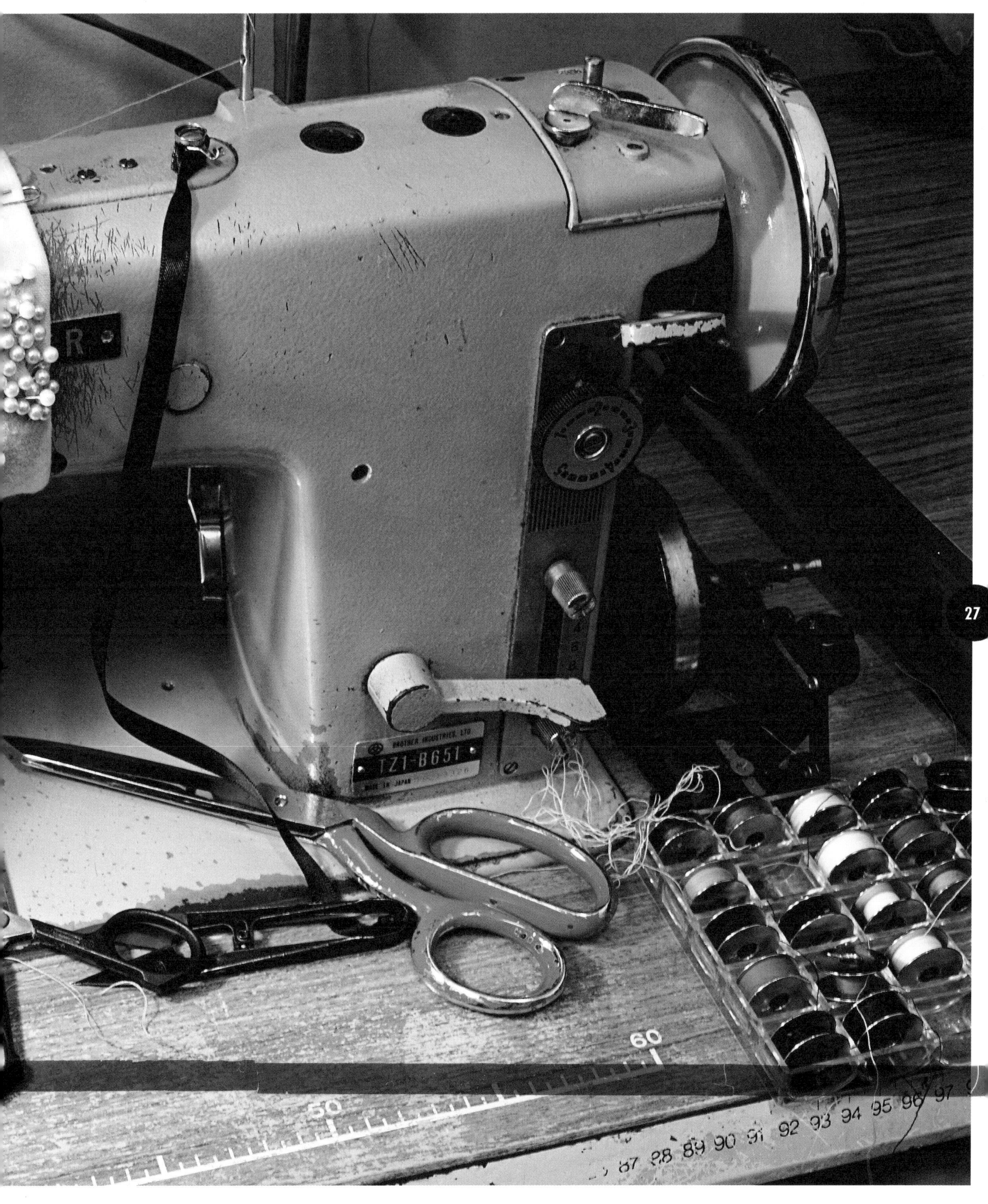

associated with the church – candles, religious giftware, ecclesiastical silverware, rosary beads, crucifixes and statues of saints. It doesn't sell books, although it does stock a few Bibles. 'You need to know theology to stock books,' says Claire de Muth. 'We leave it to the experts.'

On the day we visit Church Stores, in a corner of the shop, western traditions meld and collide with another form of ancient symbolism. Draped on a mannequin is a red and gold chasuble, a loose-fitting robe worn over a white alb. The front of the chasuble is traditional – rich red fabric edged with red and gold brocade decorated with crosses. The back is a shock, and hilarious – traditional in form, but with a circular embroidered badge in the centre, featuring the profile of a crocodile, a couple of teeth showing, surrounded by a border of yam vine leaves. It's a special order for an island community in the Torres Strait, the crocodile being the symbol the locals have used for the island for thousands of years, the yam vine its plant. The badge, about the size of a drinks coaster, was machine embroidered by a freelancer who works off-site. All the embroidery is done by machine these days in this country – it would be too expensive to have it done by hand, says Claire de Muth. When her father-in-law had Church Stores, there were four embroiderers working full-time for the company. 'Those skills were lost in the late Sixties. They still exist in Europe – they have the population there to cover it.'

Behind the chasuble are shelves of linens from Ireland, and opulent silks, and braids and cords, imported from England, Europe and New York. Materials you could imagine, sacrilegiously, in a very different setting, as upholstery and cushions in luxury hotels. Brocades and damasks with ecclesiastical designs of grapes and crosses woven into them, and in rich purples, reds, greens, golds and whites. 'The traditional colours,' says Claire de Muth. 'Purple in solemn times such as Lent, green reflects growing so that's used throughout the year, white or gold are for the joyous celebratory period of Christmas, and red is for the Spirit.'

In a narrow back room at Church Stores, these fabrics and far more modest materials are being made up into garments by two vestment makers, with two tailors working off-site. Brother sewing machines are threaded up. A bookshelf – the staff library – contains, among other paperbacks, *Angela's Ashes* and *The Da Vinci Code*. Boxes of handmade patterns, dating back years, are on the windowsill.

There's an element of fashion to the garments, says Helen Faulks. 'From time to time, things change. In the Seventies and Eighties there was a great shift towards more modern ecclesiastical designs.' The motif work varied, and shapes changed. But with an expected 10 to 15 years' wear out of an often worn garment, and 50 or even 100 years out of some of the pieces only worn on ceremonial occasions, any changes are minimal so as not to become dated.

Men make up the bulk of Church Stores' clientele, although, with an increasing number of women in the clergy, this is starting to change. 'There's no great difference in the vestments,' says Helen Faulks. 'Maybe a dart here and there, and buttons right over left instead of left over right. Women clergy are very interested in the ins and outs of the process – they're always a great deal of fun to work with.'

There's only one group of women Church Stores never makes garments for – nuns. Not many orders use habits anymore, says Helen Faulks. 'And the ones that do make their own – usually that's the task of one of the members of the order.' And those women who spend their lives sewing for the sisters often, she says, 'also make habits worn by the brothers, and for priests as well'.

Pianos

Wayne Stuart takes us into the fabric-padded studio at the Stuart Pianos factory. There's a seriousness about the room, an absolute silence. One doorway leads towards the factory, with its machinery and tools, the cabinet-makers and carpenters, the spray-painters and wood machinists, the other towards the mundane office. A quartet of pianos is lined up, each one in an unexpected shade of Australian timber – honey-coloured huon pine, one with decorative inlay panels; a cedar one, another a rich bronze. No black pianos in sight. The timber for the Stuart pianos comes from suppliers around Australia. The hefty metal frame is made in a foundry not far from the Stuart Pianos factory in Newcastle. Almost all the other components of the pianos, including the strings, are made in the factory, which was once a veterinary supplies warehouse, and stands on a bleak residential street in the New South Wales industrial port city.

A national magazine recently featured the Stuart piano as one of the 20 Australian design triumphs of the past 20 years, and had it being made 'in a small workshop in a converted church in the centre of Newcastle'. It may once have been, but, anyway, it's

tempting to romanticise anything to do with musical-instrument making. Newcastle seems an unlikely spot for a piano factory; for a while research was being carried out on the piano at Newcastle University, but even Wayne Stuart admits it's not a town where you'd expect to find a piano maker, and is not always the easiest place to be. 'It has all the potential in the world, but the infrastructures aren't here.'

When he sits down at a Stuart piano to show us how it sounds, we're expecting something avant garde – maybe some Ligeti or Elliott Carter; something as new as the piano itself. Instead, Wayne Stuart bashes out a singalong tune, rippling and showy.

It's a tune he would have played as a teenager in the country halls of Tasmania (or Van Diemen's Land, as he prefers to call it) as part of an old time dance band. There was no piano in the Stuart house in northern Tasmania when he was a young kid, 'but there were pianos everywhere. They were all over the place. My sister had lessons, and I wanted lessons but of course it wasn't the done thing for a boy. We used to work in the fields to earn money. I said to dad "I want to learn the piano and I'm jolly well going to save up and pick beans", or peas or whatever it was that summer.' He learnt to play by ear, and did eventually get lessons.

Wayne Stuart liked the old songs, had a good memory at the time and fancied himself as a bit of a performer. He picked up very quickly 'how to get around the bloody keyboard' and by the time he joined the dance band, he could play for four hours from memory. 'Anything from barn dances to old time waltzes. "Pride of Erin", all that huge wad of music written from 1900 to 1950. Lots of American music, Irish music, old ballads and that stuff.'

By the time he was 16, he estimates he would have played 100 pianos or more. 'From all different countries – French, English, American, Australian and any other one you can think of.' Some were good, some were all right, some were terrible. Each, he says, follow national characteristics – the American, for instance, is 'very bright, with a good strong sound – very typical of everything you'd think about America'. The French is more subtle.

Wayne Stuart realised early on he'd never be a concert pianist; 'I had a burning desire, a passion, to play, but I was more interested in the mechanical side of things.' He comes from a family of six children – all used to make something or other. One brother used to make billycarts, another made cannons. 'If you lost a finger, what the hell – it was great experimentation, how life should be.' Wayne Stuart made 'musical instruments with strings on them, little harp things. I was interested in the guts of the piano.' He was one of the few boys in Australia who wanted to be a piano builder. And if he was going to be a piano builder, his pianos were going to be different from anyone else's, he decided. 'There's no point in doing it otherwise.'

To the outsider, there's something bold, arrogant or even slightly mad about an Australian wanting to build a new version of an instrument that's been around for hundreds of years and, essentially, hasn't changed for at least a century. 'I can understand why people would think that, but if you're writing a book, you're certainly not writing the first book ever written.' Certain people, he says, 'have some inkling of their destiny – I think most people do if they're honest about it. I knew I wasn't going to be run of the mill, I was quietly determined.'

Stuart pianos do sound different from other pianos. Wayne Stuart talks about two- and three-dimensional sound, of horizontal and vertical sound, the vertical colour of sound. Stuart pianos, he says, have vertical sound – transparent sound, a sound that carries and has greater sustain than some of the more well known pianos. It may be a hard concept for the non-musician to grasp – as one friend put it, though, after she'd first heard a Stuart piano, 'I couldn't believe how it sounded – it's like they'd tied down a bunch of bellbirds under the bonnet.'

'The ear needs constant stimulation,' says Wayne Stuart. 'If the piano still has a place in Western culture, it's got to excite people, it has to change. That's my fundamental belief.' It certainly isn't everyone's belief – a lot of people think the piano sounds just fine as it is, and concert halls around Australia are still buying Steinways. He talks about the ear being the organ of fear. 'Its primary function is to determine if you're safe or if there are potential dangers around. The eye is not so attuned. If you're going to change an instrument that a culture perceives as safe you're going to be prepared for a fight. It's not easy, you're going against tradition.'

The Stuart piano, he says, is not played in the same way as the standard piano, 'which you just hit – they've been made to produce the best sound with the most appalling technique, with any technique at all. With our pianos, if the pianist is nervous, you'll hear everything. You hear the mental state of the pianist and that frightens people.'

Shoes for the Moscow Circus

It's taken a lifetime of work – and help from a large number of people, including university and TAFE departments and business partner Robert Albert of the music company J. Albert & Son – for Wayne Stuart (whose wife, Katie, works with him as do, at times, their two sons) to come up with his piano design which, to the outsider, superficially looks just like any other grand piano both from the outside and under the lid. A major part of the difference comes from the way the strings are held against the hammer strike – in a traditional piano, the strings are held horizontally, in the Stuart piano a device holds them vertically, in the same direction as the hammer strike, which gives the clarity and longer sustain. In addition, the Stuart piano has more notes than the standard piano – 97, or even 102, to the more usual 88 – and an additional pedal, which gives the pianist greater control over the intensity of the hammer strike.

There's nothing completely new in his pianos – it's just the way Wayne Stuart has managed to put it all together in a modern instrument. The vertical coupling, for instance – a Eureka moment, he says, when he first thought of it during the early Eighties – was done by a number of French, English and American piano makers in the mid-nineteenth century before most switched to the simpler horizontal approach. There were pianos with the same size keyboard as the Stuart being built in the 1840s – and music written for that greater range – until they, too, went out of fashion.

His ideas on exactly what sort of piano he wanted to design started forming early on in his training at the Sydney Conservatorium of Music as a piano technician. It was the early Seventies, and a time when the experimental contemporary music scene was relatively vibrant. 'I heard some wonderful concerts, and it was obvious the vertical colour, the physics of sound, was the driving force for contemporary compositions.' During his studies in Australia (and later in Japan and Europe), he found out as much as he could about pianos. His 'old style' training, too, he says, gave him the skills and capacity to understand everything from the drawing board through. 'They haven't trained people like that for a long time.'

It's hard to imagine a more complicated instrument – this hits home, more than anything, when you see individual keys being made by hand. Each one is different from the next and accurate to a fraction of a millimetre, and what you see on the keyboard, topped with acrylic resin from Germany, is just a tiny part of the timber key, each one of which, in its complex form, stretches well into the body of the piano. Tiny pieces

of the finest deerskin – 'it's nice and soft, and very consistent, cowskin is as rough as guts' – are attached to the keys to cushion the hammers, to stop them bouncing. The felt of each hammer is fluffed out with a needle to make it the right consistency. Like most of the factory, the area where the keys are made is quiet, with much of the work carried out with hand tools. In another area, the metal frame is being polished to make it perfectly smooth. Cabinet-makers and wood machinists, who, otherwise, would probably be working for the kitchen industry, handle the rare timbers used for the outer cases of the piano.

Lying on shelves in a temperate part of the building are sheets of veneer of *Acacia microsperma* and casuarina and 'as rare as hen's teeth' sassafras, the colour of parchment. Spools of stainless steel wire are ready to be made into piano strings, spun on a machine, stretched and straightened and wound around the core wire. 'The clear direct bass sound is from the stainless steel,' says Wayne Stuart. 'We pioneered the use of that – normally it's copper.'

Wayne Stuart doesn't think much of other pianos and piano makers – 'insurmountable shite…terrible quality…completely prostituted…bloody rubbish'. He's not interested, he says, in having his pianos in either concert halls or in Europe. 'It's a waste of time – these things are possible but not a priority.' Instead, from his Newcastle headquarters, and with a staff of about 12, around 10 pianos a year are now made – each one takes about a year to build – which are sold to private individuals around the world. He used to make fewer, but selling 10 a year is enough to cover costs, to make a profit. He's comfortable making that many. Wayne Stuart could make a piano from start to finish if he had to, 'but I'm not doing it anymore, it's too hard'. He made the first one in 2001 himself. When we visit the factory, the 54th Stuart piano is being built.

Sending them overseas is one of the easiest parts of the operation. 'We crate them here, they go down to Sydney and can be in New York the next day. It doesn't cost much – about half the cost of a bloody business class ticket.'

Bicycles

Darrell McCulloch is getting married the day after we meet him. When he drops it into the conversation, it's such a throwaway line we think he's joking. 'I'm more nervous in the back of a team car at a world championship or the Olympic Games, because if there's a puncture, I have to do a very sweet wheel change,' he says. 'It's a race against the clock, every second's important. The world's TV cameras are on me. Touch wood, I've never had to get out of the team car in a time trial at a world championship or the Olympic Games.' And anyway, it's not a big wedding, he says.

Darrell McCulloch makes bicycles. He makes them out of the garage underneath his house. You get the wrong idea when you click onto his website – it looks as if he's got a factory. Or maybe that's what you imagine, because it's hard to believe anyone can be 'the best bicycle maker in Australia, by a mile' as someone who knows put it, by working purely out of his garage. 'Prepare to be underwhelmed,' he tells his clients when they say they're planning to drop in on him in the Brisbane cul-de-sac.

The setting might be uninspired, but even to someone whose bike-riding career ended at the age of 10, Llewellyn steel-framed bikes (named after his middle name) are spectacular looking objects, and it's not surprising to hear there's a waiting list of nine months to acquire one. His bicycles are custom-made, each one perfectly formulated for the individual rider – to fit their body (using information gathered during a full biomechanical assessment, usually by an Australian Institute of Sport expert), to suit their needs, whether that be to train several hundred kilometres each week, to race in the velodrome, to go on road trips around Europe or to 'put their bike on the top of the black BMW, drive down to Park Road, do a lap of the river and sit in a coffee shop. That's not cycling to me, but you can't discriminate.'

Hopefully he can give that last lot something, he says. 'You can go into the whole psychology of it – I know people who completely change their lives and on the way I don't think they've ever really loved doing something except what's on the bottom line. They have the black BMW to keep up with the friend with the black Audi but then I've seen them get a bicycle and start to love it. It might be the endorphins, but five or 10 years later, I've seen them become really passionate about something, and it's less about the image and more about the doing and enjoying and sharing. Maybe the bicycle can help them find love in some way, and they probably find their personal life goes better as well – who knows.'

Spend time with Darrell McCulloch and you find much of the talk about bicycles drifts into areas not directly associated with the bike frame itself. There's a lot of time to think when you're riding 75 kilometres a day, as he does most mornings, or 'chopping and grinding and filing' in the garage for a full day, with the radio on ABC Radio National 'for feeding my brain' or ABC Classic FM or, at certain times of the year, the cricket. 'It's lovely, I love the cricket, I absolutely love it.' He also loves steam trains – he belongs to a club and is building a working scale model of one in his workshop. It may take years. 'That's my other passion – but when I knock off from bikes, I don't want to work on the loco.'

Darrell McCulloch works alone. Depending on the complexity of the bike detailing, it can take him up to 250 hours to build a frame. He has no intention of taking on helpers. 'It would be like commissioning 12 people to paint Turner paintings.' Not that he's suggesting he's an artist – 'Art's something hang on the wall to admire; bikes get used' – it's more that he can stay in control of every aspect of production and spend time talking to clients. 'When you start employing people, the whole thing gets destroyed; you end up with a factory. You lose the details that go into the frame.'

There's a certain inevitability to Darrell McCulloch's life in bicycles. He grew up in a family that didn't have a car, only had bikes, and one of his first memories at about the age of three was of a 'big box coming through the back door of the family home and Dad not opening it. I must have known what was inside it and kicked up such a stink that he relented. It was a blue Cyclops tricycle – from then on that was it.' He wished he still had it, but the thing collapsed when he sat on it about 15 years later, trying to race his young sister. 'I do have photos of me cleaning and polishing it. I looked like a team mechanic even when I was four years old.'

He remembers learning to ride a two-wheeler, 'going round and round the house and yard, up the hill and back down, skidding into the corner and occasionally overshooting and hitting the fence. And then the first time I rode on the road – it was so easy to pedal on the hard road after the grass. From then on, it was bikes all the way.'

Good at woodwork and metalwork at school, he had thought about becoming a watchmaker, but a careers adviser told him it was a dead end because watches were all going digital. 'That's wrong, it's another little niche market and there can be a 10-year waiting list for wind-up watches.' He also contemplated joining the Air Force to work on aircraft, but happened to read an article in a bike magazine about an American team mechanic, 'and the hotels he stayed in, the hardships. That really changed me.'

He started bike racing, and left school to work with frame builder Eric Hendren at Hoffy Cycles at Sandgate, a shop that's been there since 1928. He stayed for six and a half years, learning as much as he could before moving on a couple of times, and eventually started making his own frames, very much as a part-time venture.

At first, he did it all out of a tiny space in his parents' garage. His first Llewellyn frame was for Blair Stockwell, who he was working for at Lifecycle in Brisbane. 'It was a training bike, done as a job to get the jigging and everything else sorted out. He used it for many years. That was bike 001.' All Llewellyn bikes are numbered – when we visit, he's working on number 360.

For years Darrell McCulloch travelled around the world, racing for part of the year, making frames in Australia for a few months at a time, working as a team

CONTRÔLE ANTI-DOPAGE
Drug test office
Kontroll Enepdopin

mechanic, largely in Europe, for various men's and women's cycling teams. 'It's a lifestyle I didn't want to continue because the frame building was always calling.'

And so for several years he has been making one frame at a time in his basement workshop. There's no time saving, he says, on working on a few frames at once. 'Each is a little bit different – if you're offering a stock model you can build batches of things, but I'd get bored doing that.'

At every step of the bicycle-building process, the frame is meticulously checked on an alignment table – with its almost perfectly flat cast-iron surface – to make sure 'I keep everything A-one'. He very rarely has to do any corrections of the 'main triangle' of the bike, he says. 'You just take your time, do it right, with no stresses.'

His is a business that has benefited from the rise of the internet – he ships frames to England and the United States. When we're there, an enquiry comes in from Sweden. And technology, too, helps in that as he's making a bicycle, he takes a photograph of it every night on a digital camera and emails it to its owner. Apart from that, technology hasn't made any difference to the business, he says, surrounded by the most old-fashioned of tools, the most standard of machinery.

Unlike many bikes these days which are made out of carbon fibre, the basic frame of a Llewellyn bicycle is steel tubing, which comes in 'multitudes of different types'. It doesn't come in long lengths, cut to size, as you might imagine if you don't know much about bicycle making, but rather 'it all has variable wall thickness, with the ends of the tube thicker than the middle. You choose the wall thickness and diameter to suit the client, to suit the kind of bike they want.'

The tubing is held together by stainless steel lugs, many of which Darrell McCulloch has designed himself. It's these that can be the most spectacular part of a Llewellyn bike – and with the many hours taken to work with them, can add thousands to the cost of a bike. There's no reason for them to stand out, but many of the people who now buy his bikes want those details to feature – to have those lugs cut and shaped into elaborate designs like pieces of goth jewellery, to have hearts and arrows cut into them, for them to be filed and sanded right down over about an hour and a half, finally using a thousand grit sandpaper that feels like silk, to give the stainless steel a mirrored shine. Darrell McCulloch is proud of his lugs. He only designs them if they need designing – no need to reproduce anything that's available anywhere else – and he sells

MADE IN SWEDEN
5
4

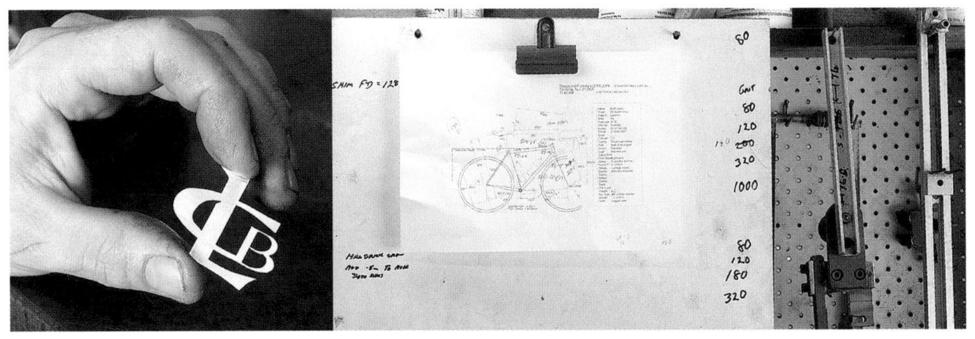

them to frame makers all over the world. ‘Lug construction was the way frames were made for 100 years, but it started to die out because everyone was in mortal combat to make products cheaper and cheaper and faster and faster.’ He uses molten silver to join the lugs and tubing – carefully letting it flow into the joint to form a solid seal. Look closely at a joint and sandwiched between the frame and the stainless steel lug is a fine and even ring of the precious metal. Silver becomes molten at a lower temperature than other metals, he says, meaning less chance of distortion of the steel parts.

It’s most likely the lugs that helped one of his bikes get Best in Show at the international bicycle exhibition, Cirque, in 2007. Even without knowing a thing about bikes, you can appreciate the beauty of the lean, red machine, with brake cables that disappear into the steel tubing, a streamlined polished steel plate over the spot where that happens, a tiny spot of solder where spokes cross, no detail or element that looks extraneous or out of place. It’s a bike that has never been on the road. ‘It’s done a lap around the conference centre in Portland, Oregon, and that’s all. It sounds a bit pretentious but collectors will go nuts over a bike like this in 10 or 20 years’ time.’ Whether it has any value is not important, though: ‘It’s nice to keep a bike to show what I could build at the height of my knowledge of the craft at the time, circa 2007. I’m keeping it.’

The wheels on Llewellyn bikes are made by Darrell McCulloch. Not all wheels are made by frame makers – many come ready-made. ‘Years ago, all wheels were hand built,’ he says. The rims for his come from a factory down the road in Brisbane, the spokes, in different gauges and lengths, are imported from Switzerland. 'These wheels you bust a spoke and you can re-rim it tomorrow from a good wheel builder anywhere in the world, and be out on the road again. You can use it for 10 years without a problem.'

Llewellyn bikes are built to last, says Darrell McCulloch. 'Twenty years, no trouble. The modern market's not so much about that, it's about changing this year's ringtone sound. The old saying is "fashion is such an ugly form you have to change it every year". I like to make a bike that people ride, that gives them longevity and durability, that gives them more value every year.'

A multimillionaire client is still riding the Llewellyn bike he bought in 1992. 'I saw him on it four weeks ago – to me, he "gets" it.' Darrell McCulloch himself doesn't have any more bikes than he needs – 'a weekend bike I ride in all weathers and a fixie [fixed wheel bike] which I rode this morning through slush. I've gone 10 years without building myself a bike. As long as it's working, it's about cycling, it's not about "have a look at my machine".' The primary aim when actually making the bike, he says, 'is to try and do better than I did last week'.

There are mottos above Darrell McCulloch's desk. He reads one, a printout from an internet forum, out loud. 'Frame builders, I always thought and said, answer to a higher calling. If they didn't, they'd be more in tune with the market, more apt to worry about trends, concerned with the time clock…Most frame builders build frames to build frames – if they finally perfect the gig, there'd be no effing reason in the world to come in and continue.'

Millet Brooms

A few days before our visit to the Tumut Broom Factory, I saw a man sweeping the footpath with a millet broom. Or not so much saw the man, I heard him sweeping. It's a sound I hadn't heard for years, and it's like waves – the opposite in every way to the whine of the leaf blower that's too often outside my window. I almost said something to the man with the broom, but decided against it.

The Tumut Broom Factory – a long low shed – is opposite the Old Butter Factory. The visitors' centre is now in the butter factory. There's not much farming left around Tumut; timber's the main industry of the area.

At one time 120 families in the area, as far out as Gundagai, grew millet; all up, there would have been around 1000 hectares planted with it. It's a special kind of millet – white Italian broom millet that grows as tall as the rafters in the broom factory – and it was grown from the 1920s onwards as a cash crop to complement the dairy farming over the summer months. At its peak, about 1200 tonnes were harvested around Tumut. Now, it only grows on about two or three farms, and they'd be lucky to grow eight tonnes.

'There are about 20 different varieties of millet that we know of,' says Geoff Wortes, who runs the broom factory with Rob Richards. Geoff's father, Cliff, started there a few months after it opened in 1946 and stayed until his retirement. Geoff Wortes and Rob Richards, who both grew up in Tumut, worked there on and off when they were young, eventually coming back to take over the place in the early Nineties.

Something like 75 per cent of Australia's millet used to grow in the Tumut area and virtually everyone in town would be involved around harvest time. The soil's right for millet, and so is the climate. 'The autumn months are mild – that's the harvest period, March to May,' says Geoff Wortes. 'The rule of thumb was that you'd plant your crop on Melbourne Cup Day, and then it would be a 90-day growing period.' The planting would be staggered – from early October to early December, to spread the harvest over two months.

You'd want to stagger the harvest – it's not the sort of work anyone could do quickly. It all has to be done by hand, as the millet's too tall to be mechanically harvested. Geoff Wortes drags out some old photos of millet harvesting – a man, probably quite a big man, looks the size of a thumb in between two rows of corn-like crops. Before it can be cut, there's the 'tabling' of the millet, as it's called. 'It's a job that suits big burly front rowers,' says Geoff Wortes. 'It's good exercise.' The bloke moves down the rows, grabs an armful of millet from one row and bends it down, an armful from the other and throws it down on top and so it goes, like plaits, down the paddock, forming a 'table' over the rows. And when it's all been tabled, which could take hours, he, or someone else, goes back and slices through the thick armfuls of millet with a pocket knife 'sharp enough to shave the hairs off your arm'. Those bundles are spread out and lie on the table for a few days to start drying out, and are then gathered up and tied and hung to dry in a shed on the farm. Lots of farms around Tumut had drying sheds for millet. You can still see a few in the area.

Depending on the weather, the millet dries in about three weeks. If it's raining, it can go black with mould or stain the colour of rust. Before anyone was worried about pollution, those stains would be removed with bleach, and the town would stink of rotten eggs. Now, around half the millet comes in from Mexico. 'We'll take all the local millet we can, but can't justify running a business on two or three local growers,' says Geoff Wortes. 'If they have a bad year, we're out of business.' So as well as stained millet, a bad year can produce wavy stalks. No one knows why that happens – the millet looks as if it's had a bad perm, and is no good for the outside of a broom. A few stalks can go deep within the broom, where no one will see them, but you wouldn't want too many. 'One year, 50 per cent of the crop was like that – it's waste. You work on 25 per cent being waste, depending on the year.'

There were broom factories all over Australia at one time. The Federal Broom Factory in Sydney, factories in Victoria, a factory run by the deaf and dumb in South Australia. 'There would have been about 14 of them,' says Geoff Wortes. There's only one today. The Tumut millet would be bought individually from the farms by the factories, at the mercy of the auctioneers in Sydney and Melbourne. In 1946 the farmers got together and formed a co-operative, and 'within two years the price of millet went up from £7 a ton to £200 a ton – it was a successful move. All the buyers and factories had to buy through the co-op.'

The co-op set up the broom factory, selling to hardware stores and stock and station agents around Australia, New Zealand and New Guinea, with a few government contracts as well. 'The government contracts weren't worth a lot financially – they'd argue over a halfpenny – but kept you going,' says Geoff Wortes. His father told him that in one railway contract that bought by weight, 'instead of using ash handles which were commonly used in brooms, they'd use spotted gum because it was considerably heavier. That way you'd pick up your halfpenny.' When it was going all out, the factory was making up to 500 brooms a day, employing six broom makers at piecework rates, with a staff of around 12 or 15 all up. Nowadays, the factory would average 10-12,000 brooms a year. 'Some days we make 50, other days we go fishing.'

The factory only had about 15 years of being prosperous – by the early Sixties every housewife wanted a vacuum cleaner. 'The broom was something you worshipped in the house before vacuum cleaners.' As well, cheap brooms started coming in from overseas. In the hard years, the Tumut Broom Factory reduced the operation to only about three workers. 'That's one reason we've kept going – these days, you're either our size cottage industry or you're huge.'

Geoff Wortes and Rob Richards, plus a casual worker who comes in two or three days a week, make brooms the way they have always done. It's the same way that millet brooms are made everywhere in the world, says Geoff Wortes. Some machines

EXIT

in the factory are from the United States; a Power Broom Machinery catalogue from 1903, with an embossed cover, is from Syracuse, New York. 'You look at the old movies – they've all got a broom in them,' says Geoff Wortes.

In the back room of the factory there's a sorting machine, and a long bench, where millet is sorted by hand. Geoff Wortes sorts a bundle as if he's shuffling and dealing cards at a blackjack table – fast, into smaller bundles of different lengths and different quality, repeating the process again and again until he's satisfied with the result. 'Usually a man going flat out here for six hours can keep your broom-maker going for eight – that's when you're good at it. In the old days it was all sorted by hand, we didn't have a machine.'

He doesn't have to sort the Mexican millet – it comes in hessian sacks, all ready. The local millet still has a few seeds on it, which are beaten out in the threshing machine, a steel drum with protruding knife-like attachments. A few seeds are not necessarily a bad thing. As Geoff Wortes tells it, in 1790 Abraham Lincoln was sent a whisk broom from France to brush his top hat. One seed was on that whisk broom. He planted it in his garden to see what it was. 'That was the beginning of the broom industry in America.' You can find other stories of how the US broom industry started, but that one's the best.

Six types of broom are made at the Tumut Broom Factory, four less than they used to. They used to have names like Jumbuck and Parlour and Sweepeasy. They didn't make 10 grades of broom because anyone asked for 10 different brooms. It was to minimise factory waste – millet came in different lengths and qualities from the farms, and so they'd make brooms accordingly.

When there were lots of broom factories around, the Tumut Broom Factory used to make a Number One Special broom with a piece of rag around the handle 'to make it stand out against our opponents, to dress it up for the housewives. That was our marketing edge – it didn't make them sweep any better.'

Now the brooms are called things like Woolshed, Six Tie, Caravan Broom and Toy Broom, and mainly sold through stock and station agents in the country. The caravan and toy brooms are clever ways of using up the shortest millet. The Woolshed, for shearing sheds, stables and building sites, has split cane through the millet 'to give a heavier sweep – it's a bit more of a bloke's broom, I suppose'.

There are no scales or weights at the Tumut Broom Factory – everything's measured by hand. After a few years of working with millet, 'you get the feel of how much to use', says Rob Richards. A Six Tie broom has 'about three handfuls' of millet. (Six Tie refers to the number of lines of stitching across the broom.) He's at a machine making the broom, but there's nothing automated about it. The machine no more makes the brooms than a potter's wheel makes the pots – there's craft in what he does. The various grades of millet sit in boxes beside him. Working with millet, he says, can be rough on the hands, 'but they toughen up. Some millet's like bending steel, other's nice and soft.'

Rob Richards picks up a yellow broom handle, hammers in a nail close to one end of it to hold the end of a spool of thick wire which is the only thing attached to the machine. The wire wraps tightly – more tightly than it could be by hand – around the millet and keeps it in place. Building up the broom is an intricate process, starting with an inner core of the least desirable, but still A-grade millet. On either side of that is a 'shoulder' of millet, a small handful, to 'make it look as if it's standing up straight and to give a flat side to the broom – when we had apprentices, you'd often find the shoulders dropping off to one side. It's all about presentation.' Rob Richards is pounding the shoulders into shape as he goes, pulling out strands of millet he doesn't like the look of. With a butcher's knife, he shaves back the millet on the end closest to

the handle. Within minutes, more layers of millet are added, dampened at one end to make them flexible enough to bend over on themselves, the finest and straightest the outer layer, with a final twist of wire to hold the layers. He makes half a dozen brooms as I watch, and they all look as similar as any well-made handmade objects can look. 'You've got to keep your wits about you, doing this work,' says Rob Richards. 'You've got to have a good work ethic. Someone's going to pay decent money for the broom so it's no good making something that looks shoddy.'

When he's finished with the brooms, they go to the stitching machine, a massive contraption made in Baltimore in the Fifties. Geoff Wortes and his father bought it secondhand up in Rockhampton in the Seventies. With a series of hooks, needles and ratchets, the machine stitches seven lines of heavy red thread across the millet – a Seven Tie broom. The lines of stitching aren't quite even.

Ask how long a Tumut broom can last and the answer is obvious. 'It depends how often you sweep – there are some pretty manic sweepers around.' The Tumut Broom Factory has letters from 'people who say they've had their broom for 10 years – they wear them down to the strings'. They send photos too – one worn down to the strings looks like a broken tooth.

The stitching machine breaks down every now and then, and Geoff Wortes is the only person who can fix it. 'There have been newer versions, but they work on the same principle, which means you're still sitting there doing most of the work. We figure for $US70,000, we'll stick with what we know.' The nearly finished broom is trimmed by a guillotine, operated by a pneumatic pump. 'And then we bunch them up into dozens, put the labels on, put a chaff bag over them, wrap them up and off they go around the countryside. Probably most shearing sheds in Australia have got one of our brooms in them somewhere.' Hundreds of brooms are lined up at one end of the shed, ready to go, with handles of green and gold – 'Australian colours' – and a few red thrown in for variety. They smell of stables and rope.

Flagmakers

John Vaughan describes himself as a vexillographer. It's a word that Microsoft Word puts a red squiggle under to tell you you've made a spelling mistake. It's not a word that's in the Macquarie Dictionary, although it is in some other dictionaries. John Vaughan is actively trying to get it into the next edition of the Macquarie Dictionary. He's been sending emails. The first one reads: 'Dear Macquarie Dictionary Editor, I have been asked by my local *North Shore Courier* publication whether your main dictionary contains the word VEXILLOGRAPHER which is my profession as a flag historian and designer. I look forward to your response. Regards John Christian Vaughan Vexillographer.' The reply, complete with phonetic symbols, explains that there are the various parts of speech associated with vexillology, 'the systematic study of flags, their meanings, history etc' but 'no reference to a Vexillographer, just a vexillologist'.

SINGER
SEWING MACHINE COMPANY
MADE IN JAPAN

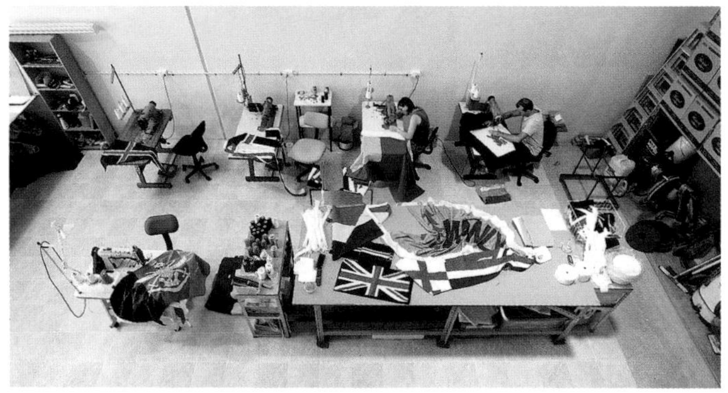

'Thank you,' replied John Vaughan. 'May I apply for the word VEXILLOGRAPHER to be included in any new edition? Cheers, John.' When we visited, he was waiting for a reply. 'The "-ographer" bit of it says you design as well as study flags.'

He's designed a number of flags – sometimes as a commission, other times unsolicited – including Sydney Ferries, the City of Willoughby (which features, among other things, a masonry crown 'representing the imaginary stone wall protecting the city of Willoughby', a quaint notion) and the Greater Sydney Ensign, 'which features the Southern Cross of 1823...on the red cross of St George with a great maritime anchor and six-pointed star, Sirius, in the centre and the HM Bark *Endeavour* in the first canton'. One of his recent design jobs was the Sydney Observatory flags – flags which show the various phases of the moon. They only fly during the daytime – it seems odd for flags to indicate a night-time only phenomenon, but a nice idea that anyone with good enough eyesight who happens to drive by in daylight hours is given the information in such an old-fashioned way.

John Vaughan should go on *The Einstein Factor*. His specialty would be flags and it wouldn't matter whether his opponents' choices were Jane Austen, butterflies or Led Zeppelin, he'd win. This is a man who knows everything there is to know about flags, and as soon as you start talking to him, he's telling you about the 32,823 entries in the Australian national flag competition in 1901, and how there were five winners (one a woman from Perth) with identical entries, how the only difference between that Australian flag and today's is the number of points on the stars. 'Star Alpha at the bottom of the Southern Cross started off with nine and it went around eight, seven, six and five, showing the brightness of stars in the sky. Of course, the Commonwealth star at that point only had six points instead of seven…then the Southern Cross was altered in 1903 to four seven-pointed stars and one five-pointer. The one five-pointer is Epsilon and that's a very small star that we even leave off the Southern Cross here in New South Wales, and the Commonwealth star, the symbol of Federation, had the seventh point added in 1908…'

It's not easy to find anywhere to sit in John Vaughan's office. The former one-bedroom flat in the shopping strip at Northbridge, on Sydney's North Shore, is full of flags. New flags, old flags, flags hanging up, in the doorway, on the shelves, flags in boxes, flags in bags and, right by the visitor's chair, Dick Smith's gigantic flag, in for repair, stuffed into a great big Australia Post mailbag. There are photos of flags on the wall, including a shot of a lifesaving carnival with the long triangular pennant of Narrabeen spelling out the name of the club in 'tapering block letters' in maroon and black. Not typical beach colours but, says John Vaughan, 'I'm a believer that a flag should stand out in the environment where it's displayed. Take for instance Norfolk Island – it's a very green place and their flag is green. The flag should be a bright, strong colour that can be seen against the physical features of the island.' He designed a more suitable flag, red, with a white circular badge in the fly – 'the flapping edge' – and the green Norfolk Island pine at the centre of the badge. 'And then in the first canton, the top end of the flag towards the masthead, we have the first union flag with the crosses of St George and St Andrew. It's widely flown on the island, too, I believe.'

A good design for a flag, says John Vaughan, who has several thousand in his private collection, has the main motif 'offset towards the hoist' – in other words closer to the flagpole – so that 'when the fly wears, you can trim off part of it, rehem it and get a second life out of the flag. When I designed the Sydney Ferries flag, I made certain the major device was in the first canton, so that even if half the flag has gone, you can still recognise the design.' Flags wear out faster than you think, he says. 'Imagine leaving your washing on the line in all weathers for months at a time, and that will give you some idea.'

John Vaughan, who worked in a bank for '20 years and three days' before concentrating on his flag business 20-odd years ago, has always been interested in flags. His father and grandfather both had flagpoles in their gardens and so does John Vaughan himself. The appeal of flags to him largely stems from an interest in history – 'a flag encapsulates the feeling of the time when it was designed' – but there's also an emotional element to it. When you see a flag blowing in 'a nice, warm nor'easter over this beautiful harbour', he says, 'it does remind you of the absolute beauty and, hopefully, tranquillity of Sydney. The flag itself represents the elements, because it moves with the wind – it provides a link with nature.'

As a teenager, he used to go on board cargo ships in Sydney Harbour. 'I'd just walk up the gangplanks and see if they had any old flags. It was the same with old buildings due for demolition – you'd often find flags tucked away in pigeonholes, as they call the storage space for flags.' And then, he says, he discovered there were a number of 'fairly ancient flagmakers still in Sydney – mainly around the Balmain area – and I visited them, E. H. Brett and Sons, and Harry West. I met some of the real characters who had been making flags for decades.' At one place, one of the workers had been at his machine for so long that the table had worn to a knife edge on the right-hand side, worn away by the amount of material that had passed over it.

John Vaughan's desk isn't likely to wear out. He does do some sewing, using a shiny black Singer sewing machine, which had belonged to his grandmother and then mother, but it's more in the area of repairs than the making of thousands of flags.

He leaves the making to others, such as Cathy Jukes, who works with her son Gary Fielmich and his wife, Sharon, plus extra workers when needed, in a light-industrial estate in Brisbane. Gary Fielmich, who trained as a builder, joined the flagmaking business when there was a slump in the construction industry, he says, and does 'all the cutting of flags and the appliqué zigzag sewing – the artistic side of it, not the straight sewing'.

It's December when we visit and flying out the front of the workshop, over the roll-a-door and providing shade from the Queensland sun is a massive Australian Christmas flag John Vaughan designed. Green and gold with the Southern Cross and Santa on it. Cathy Jukes flies an Irish-Australian flag for St Patrick's Day, another John Vaughan design, with a harp and a busty woman. Inside, a cutting table is swathed in

HMAS PLATYPUS
Australiana Flags
Tel 02 9958 3246 Fax 02 9958 2914
info@australianaflags.com.au
Vexillography
JOHN C VAUGHAN
PARKER

W·R·A·N·S
41-1947
1951-1985
W.R.A.N.S
WOMEN'S
ROYAL
AUSTRALIAN
NAVAL
SERVICE
SAMSON BRAND

fabric; underneath are rolls of red, white and blue fabric. On a shelving unit along one wall, clear plastic boxes are filled with scraps, the labels on the front with names of colours such as Crocus, Bluebird, Turquoise and Peach. Several industrial sewing machines are set up on workbenches, each with dozens of spools of coloured threads.

Unlike John Vaughan, Cathy Jukes hadn't had a thing to do with flags before she started making them. She'd always been good at sewing, and made ballet costumes for her daughters. When her children started school, she looked for a job – having not worked for 14 years, she answered an ad in the paper for a machinist.

'But there was a misprint – it said "slag machinist, experience not necessary", so I went for this job but didn't have a clue what I was going for. I thought I'd be bluffing my way – I wasn't going to let them know I didn't know what a slag machinist was.' She was, she says, relieved to see flags in the production manager's room.

The factory, at the time, had a contract, which lasted about three years, from the Department of Defence for about 30,000 Australian flags. The government, and particularly the defence forces, says Cathy Jukes, are generally the biggest consumers of flags. 'And any event or war, we'll be affected in some way. At the moment, so many flags are going over to Iraq and Afghanistan – we had to make funeral flags even before we had any casualties. That's a side of flagmaking you don't think about or want to think about – body bags and coffins are made before the war, and it's the same with coffin flags.' Coffin flags, she says, have a black edge and are slightly bigger than a normal flag 'so they drape over the coffin. Something like that I'll make sure I make them myself – I'm very particular. I expect my staff to be up to my standards, but that's expecting too much.'

At her first flagmaking job Cathy Jukes spent a fair bit of time thinking about the Union Jack, a part of the Australian flag she worked on. She had thought flags would be easy to make – 'they're just rectangles'. But then she found out that 31 pieces of fabric were used to construct the Union Jack alone. She came up with a way of making it from 11 pieces, a method she still uses today. 'Machinists were doing eight Union Jacks in a day – with the new method, they could do 25.'

It was never boring, she says, making only Australian flags. 'Because it was piece work, your goal was to make as many flags as you could – your mind stayed really active.'

In 1989 she set up her own company, and has become known around Australia. Her work's varied – looking through her filing cabinets filled with thousands of patterns (she keeps a brown paper pattern, covered in jottings on colours, stitching, fabric and other details, for every flag the company makes), you come across far more than national flags. Citigroup, Central West Credit Union, Cruising Yacht Club, Camberwell Girls' Grammar, Cornish Australian, Dangar Island, Buxton House. And Brisbane Leather Boyz – a chain features on that one. Many of the designs come in as a rough sketch or as a logo on a letterhead – a pattern's drawn up from that, using a light box and, to scale it up, an old-fashioned overhead projector.

One of the company's specialties is cutaway sections on flags – a labour-intensive task in which a motif is appliquéd onto the body of the flag, and the backing fabric carefully clipped away to let light through. It looks especially effective when the stars of the Southern Cross are created this way, she says.

But the day we visit, there are no cutaway sections on the work tables. Instead, Gary Fielmich is working on a two-yard Chinese flag. Surprisingly, a company that has sent much of its Australian flagwork to China has put in an order for just one red flag with five yellow stars. Bulk orders may go offshore but Cathy Jukes is confident there will always be room for her company. 'We're not big enough to be a threat,' she says.

Paper for Artists

Blue Lake paper is made of cotton. Cotton from old sheets and towels, tablecloths and serviettes, pillowcases. Cotton from hospitals and hotels. Maurice Wilson buys bags of it, 20 at a time, from an Adelaide laundry. Each bag holds about 20 kilograms of old napery and manchester, most starchy white but some with remnants of cigarette burns or, off-puttingly, stained in patches. And most hemmed with white thread but occasionally with, oddly, traces of dark blue or brown. The cotton comes in broad strips, too narrow to be used as sheets or towels or to resell as anything useful. These are rags.

Cotton paper can be made from bolls, straight from the plant, but Maurice Wilson is pleased to think that his paper is made from recycled material. He recycles water as much as he can, too – papermaking, at its worst, can be a water-intensive industry. 'If you say the word "papermill", people think you're going to do something terrible with water, they get a fright. I had to come up with something.'

Blue Lake Paper was set up in the early Nineties by Kelvin Smibert, a farmer, who Maurice Wilson met when they were both studying fine arts at TAFE. Papermaking was part of the course, and Kelvin Smibert decided to start the business in Mount Gambier, a town on the South Australian–Victorian border, aiming at the fine art market, which no one else in Australia was doing, 'and not worrying about the craft market'. He stuck to that, supplying to some of the best art supply shops in Australia, and selling directly to artists. Orders come over the net from England, the United States and New Zealand, as well as from around Australia. More Blue Lake paper goes to Sydney and Perth than to other Australian cities. It's not as popular in Adelaide and Melbourne. 'Some people think if it's local, it's not as good, and should be cheaper,' says Maurice Wilson. 'Maybe I'm wrong, but I don't push it locally.'

Kelvin Smibert used to experiment with paper, says Maurice Wilson. He'd try to make paper out of different things. For a while, he was using kangaroo droppings. There's still some of the paper in the workshop – it's the colour of brown paper. 'I left Kelvin to it,' says Maurice Wilson, who didn't like the smell of the brew. It wasn't bad paper, he says, and quite traditional in a way. 'In India you have elephant dung paper and even cow dung paper – any vegetable matter has cellulose content and that's what you make paper from.' Cotton, says Maurice Wilson, who'd worked at the post office for 18 years before he got into fine art and papermaking, 'is the highest form of cellulose, and that's why the best art papers will be made from it'.

When Maurice Wilson took over a few years ago, he didn't continue the line of kangaroo paper, but Kelvin Smibert's machines for making paper were part of the deal. Maurice Wilson has added to them, including his own inventions. They're ingenious, all a bit makeshift, all looking as if they were made by a farmer using whatever bits and pieces he had lying around. There's one with an old laundry tub and plastic plumbing pipes hitched to the side; another involves sheets of corrugated cardboard. One was made up using a trough from a farmyard. There's another that may contain parts from a plough – it looks like it, anyway. The way he makes paper, he says, is pretty well how a big paper factory would make it. 'The principles are the same – you try to push against them and think about how you could do it better, but you can't.'

A machine clacks away and looks like an industrial mincer. 'We call it the rag chopper because it chops rags and that's about it.' Strips of sheets and towels go

in at the top and blades slash away, turning them into scraps. Maurice Wilson does 7.2 kilograms at a time – that way he can keep the consistency of the paper constant. The white sheets and towels are used for white paper; any with stains, or coloured stitching, make warm white. Blue Lake used to make paper with paperbark in it, 'but you put things like that in and it takes forever to get out of the machines. I've made a rule that if someone wants something like that, it's sprinkled on towards the end.'

Blue Lake used to also make blue paper out of denim thread – bags of the stuff came from Bradmill 'and it was all a mass of thread as if something had gone haywire, you could never unravel it'. The company doesn't make blue paper anymore. 'People ask what you've got and then buy white. Once you start giving an artist coloured paper it restricts them. They can decide what to do with a piece of white paper, they can paint it blue if they want to.'

It takes about 15 minutes to chop up a whole batch of cotton; the pieces need to be small so they don't get tangled up in the beater of the 'hollander', the next machine. In this, the scraps of rag are mixed with water – water from the Blue Lake, the landmark Mount Gambier is famous for. The water is astonishing in summer, a shade of peacock blue. When you ask locals why, you get a different story every time. Maurice Wilson is more interested in its pH value – 8.2, acid-free, ideal for papermaking. He gets water from the Blue Lake by turning on the tap.

The hollander, another machine rigged up by Kelvin Smibert, with modifications by Maurice Wilson, churns and stamps the rags and water, transforming them into something that could be milk. He pumps it into a tank outside, but can't keep it there for long. It would go off, in the same way towels do if they stay damp for days.

The pulpy fluid is poured into the papermaking machine – gaffer tape partway up the side marks off the level the liquid should reach for the various weights of paper. Once all guides have been set in place for the dimensions of the paper, Maurice Wilson flicks a switch to allow the water to separate from the cotton, helping the process along by gently smoothing the surface with an old paint roller. Within a minute or two, much of the water has drained away, leaving a very damp, large sheet of artists' paper with a surface like felt. A concentrated jet of water trims the side, leaving a deckled edge.

The damp paper, now just stable enough to handle, is rolled between hot rollers to take more of the moisture out, and taken to a small, dark room to dry. The sheets are stacked up between sheets of corrugated cardboard (with layers of paper or felt protecting them from the non-acid-free and ripply cardboard), weighted down and blasted with warm air. Fans draw in heat from the old kitchen alongside via a hole in the wall. Maurice Wilson lights a fire in the wood-burning stove in the kitchen early in the morning 'with any wood I can find, and stoke it up during the day'.

Ingeniously, the corrugations in the cardboard funnel the air to dry the paper evenly. It's not the traditional way, says Maurice Wilson. 'That would be to hang it over a rope in a loft and let it air-dry.' He doesn't do it that way, he says, because paper has a memory. 'It dries wavy, you stick it back through the hot roller and it looks flat, but you wet it and it will go wavy again.' Dried under pressure, he says, it will stay flat whatever happens. It takes two days to dry a batch of paper. 'I'd like it to be 24 hours,' he says. 'It will be when I get some more equipment rigged up.'

Maurice Wilson knows when a sheet of paper is dry by the sound of it. 'You have to make sure it has a rattle,' he says. 'If it feels dry but doesn't rattle, you know there's too much moisture in it.' He picks up a piece in just the same way Rolf Harris picks up his wobble board and starts playing. A clear twang sets up. It's dry. A lot about papermaking for Maurice Wilson is to do with the sound and feel of it. 'I'm a feeling person so it suits me that way.'

Making paper the Blue Lake way couldn't be more labour-intensive. It's handled eight or nine times, Maurice Wilson estimates, before it's ready to be shipped out. Someone from Korea phoned him recently and wanted samples of his rag paper for a wedding that was happening a week and a half later. The order was for thousands of sheets. 'It was weird, I thought someone was having a loan of me,' he says. 'They knew it was handmade but wanted it immediately.' It couldn't be done in the shed in Mount Gambier.

'Kelvin wanted to make paper quicker and make more of it,' he says. 'I sort of step back from that, I want to get it right. If you're flogging yourself you may as well be making pencils, it wouldn't matter what you made.'

There are two types of artist, says Maurice Wilson, who still enters a couple of painting competitions a year. 'One sees a piece of paper as something to do a picture on. The others see the paper as part of the artwork, and that's how I see it. They're the ones who'll keep buying from you. The ones who see it as just something to paint on will try it once, and it doesn't matter to them. They'll find a piece of cardboard.'

Oars

It's lunchtime at Croker Oars. A few of the workers are sitting on battered chairs in the old woodworking shed. One's eating two-minute noodles, another – from the smell of it – leftovers from last night's casserole. Half a dozen dogs are standing around, watching for the odd scrap or for someone to throw a ball. In the doorway, against a rain-filled sky, is a horse. It's not after the stew. Across the paddock behind Croker's is a quiet stretch of the Manning River, its waterways threaded with oyster leases. In the fields beside the driveway, edged with farm fencing, are cattle on one side, draughthorses on the other.

In the new sheds at the factory is highly confidential high-tech equipment which, to the outsider, could be for anything, but it's been purpose-designed and built to make the best possible oars for Olympic rowers from the United States, Great Britain, Germany, Australia, China and a number of other countries; to make the best possible oars for anyone else who wants them as well. Photographs aren't allowed in the area where the main equipment is – it's probably not giving any trade secrets away to say that apart from the perfection of the gleaming metal moulds, the most unexpected element is the use of old-fashioned waxed cardboard milkshake containers – hundreds of them, printed with palm-fringed beaches, are taking up excess resin.

When Howard Croker moved his oar-making business from Sydney up to Oxley Island, near Taree on the NSW mid-north coast, in 1977, it was just him. And his tools and timber, and wife and four children. Part of the reason for the move was to save costs, 'and I was mad keen to farm'. He uses his draughthorses to plough, 'and setting the sheer of the plough is very similar to the pitch of an oar – the same degrees and angles. I steer a boat very straight, I steer the horses straight.' It hasn't always been easy, he says, juggling farming and the oar business, 'but we've always thought we were well off. If we wanted something, we'd work harder. We went travelling on the profit from watermelons – 70 tonnes got us overseas.'

Another reason for moving was to set up a rowing school. At various times of the year, the lawns running down to the river are covered in boats, as groups from high schools and rowing clubs meet for training sessions. A number of local children who have been coached at Croker Oars have won scholarships to Sydney private schools; some have made it to US universities on the strength of their rowing skills.

Howard Croker built the first shed with thick, tree-trunk posts and corrugated iron roof. When we visited Croker Oars, it was about to be demolished to make room for more suitable housing for the technology used in the business now – old wooden boats and oars were being taken down from the rafters, a new home found for the redundant tools. Howard Croker's house is a few steps away. In the early days, the concrete floor of the shed would be littered in wood shavings, and Howard Croker would be fit just from working the timber. He's still fit from rowing 10 kilometres three mornings a week and, now, from walking up steep slopes, in training to walk the Kokoda Trail a few months' time after our visit – 'I'm doing the things I didn't have time to do earlier on' – but making oars isn't the hard physical work it used to be.

When John Corbett turned up at Croker Oars in 1982, he'd been rowing to a high level in New Zealand and doing maintenance on the oars at his local rowing club. 'I came to visit this factory and never got away.' Between the two of them, they'd make 400 oars a year, maximum, 'and we were working really hard at the time'.

There's a pragmatic side to Howard Croker. The fact that he makes oars is testament to that. His father, a rowing coach, started him rowing at a young age; for years, he was one of the top 12 rowers in the country. The only things he was good at at school, he says, were PE and woodwork. 'I saw my class teacher, who's 94 now, at a reunion a few months ago and he said, "Howard, you were dumb." I can't say my ABC but I've always been street smart.' He left school at 15 to take up an apprenticeship as a boatbuilder, and started concentrating on oars after a couple of years. 'It wasn't that I wanted to make oars – no one likes making them. They're a hassle, boring and physically hard work. It's the low end of boatbuilding, like draining and plumbing is to building, but I could see a future in it.' He started his own company as a teenager, working out of his parents' backyard in the Sydney suburb of Ryde. 'As a kid, I remember clearly I didn't want idiots telling me what to do.'

That was in 1962: orders started coming in immediately 'and I haven't had a spare day since'. Some of his first customers were members of State and Olympic teams – contacts he'd made when he repaired their oars during his apprenticeship. When the business was too big for the backyard, he bought land on the Parramatta River, and broadened his oar making to include oars for various types of boats, including sculling oars, and surf oars for a New Zealand club. The company got a boost when Croker oars were used by the silver medal-winning Australian eight at the 1968 Olympic Games.

In the past 20 years at Croker Oars, timber has largely made way for carbon fibre. It took only two years for the changeover – the Americans had had a monopoly on the global market for carbon fibre oars during the Eighties, and Australia was slow to catch up. But when it did, it moved fast and improved rapidly – so much so that Croker Oars is now a player in the field, making around 15,000 oars a year, with a workforce of 25, and exporting to dozens of countries. Exports account for about 80 per cent of Croker's business. And instead of having to hand-carve each oar, with the potential for error, they now appear, perfectly formed from a mould, and controlled by computer technology, from the drawing stage onwards.

'My whole life could be on a memory stick,' says John Corbett. 'It's quite sad really.' Not that he's nostalgic for timber oars, around a dozen of which are still made every year. 'The good old days weren't very good at all, the equipment wasn't very good – and with timber a diminishing resource, I'd rather the spruce go to make a guitar back than get smashed to pieces out the back of a surf boat.'

Even if you know nothing about rowing, the blade of a Croker oar looks lethal, in the way a shark's tail looks lethal – its slender and rigid form designed to move through the water cleanly, quietly and very efficiently.

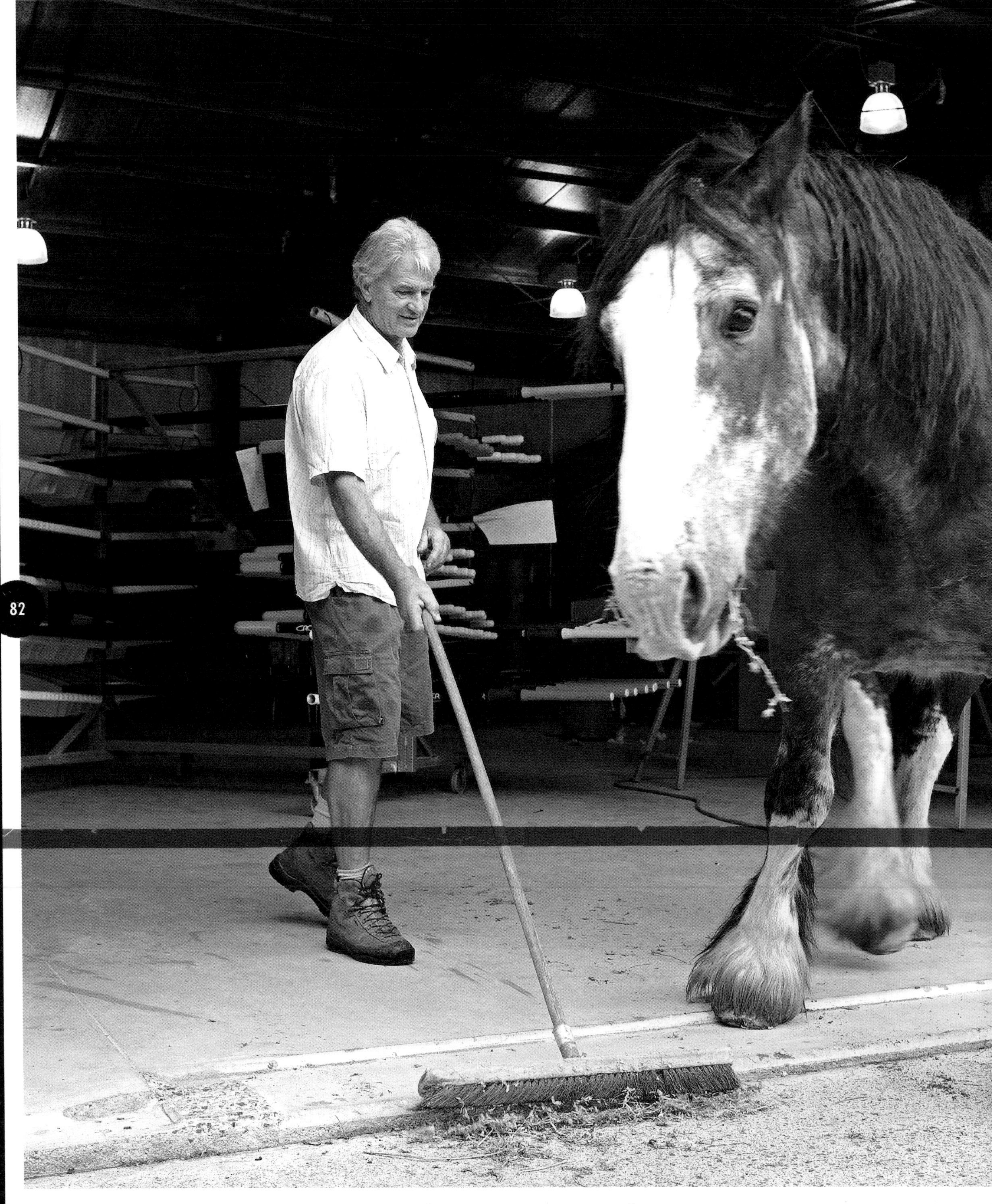

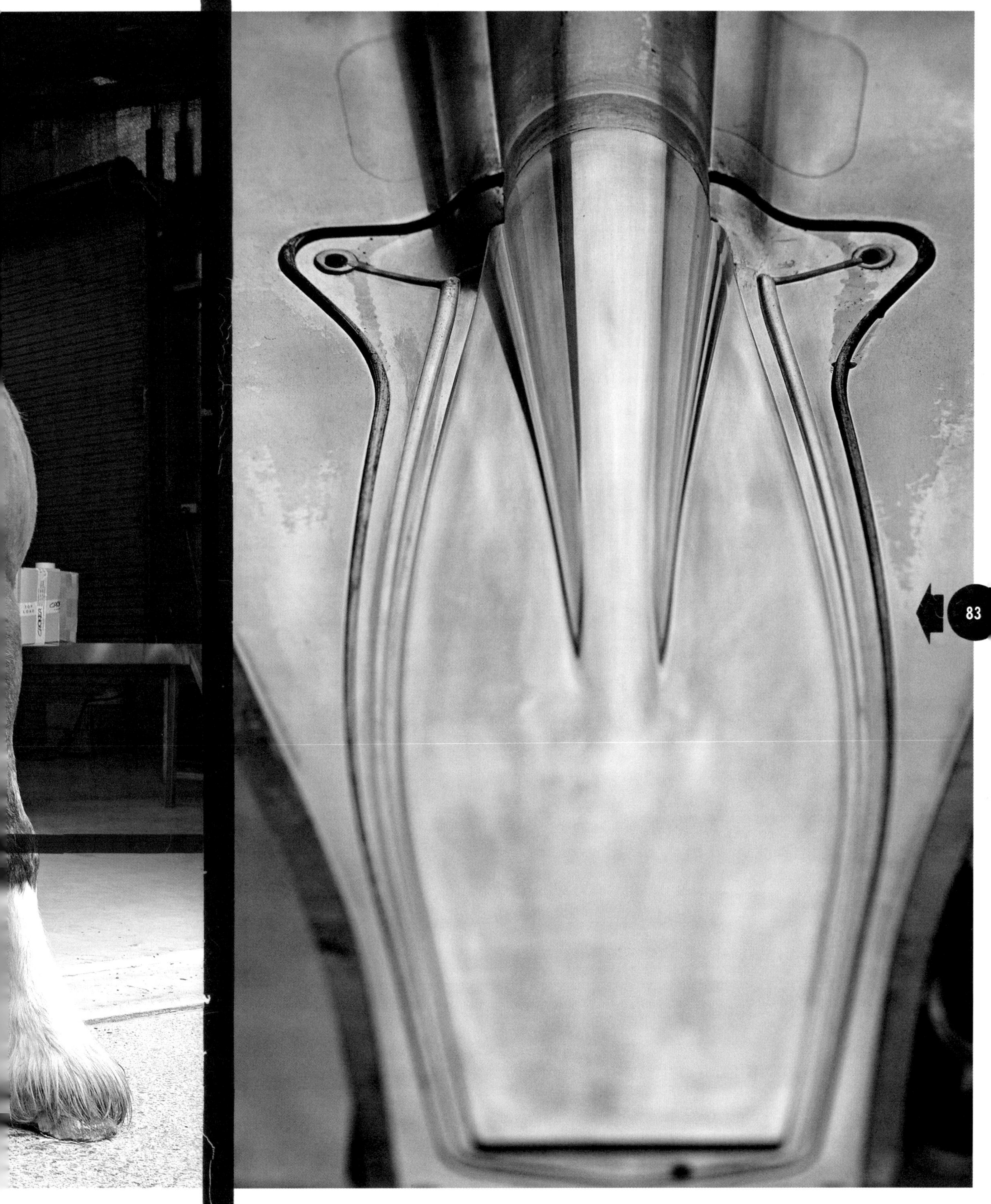

As much as possible, every part of a Croker oar is made in Australia, although that's becoming more and more difficult as toolmaking and pattern making are increasingly going offshore. 'I hate talking about having anything done in China,' says Howard Croker. 'I'll try to get everything done here for as long as I can. Toolmaking is the basis of this country – if you want to make anything, you need a toolmaker.'

Paper and pencils aren't used anymore for designing – one unexpected bonus of computer technology was that when a new sleeve design was being drawn up on screen, it came up in a lurid pink. Somehow right through the pattern stage and into final production that pink stayed, and is now associated more than anything with Croker Oars. Flick through a rowing magazine and in ads for boats and editorial shots of competitions, you can't help noticing Croker oars. 'We haven't had to advertise,' says John Corbett.

Watching the Olympic Games rowing on television several months after visiting the factory, the fluorescent pink sleeves of Croker oars stand out against the soupy Beijing atmosphere. The pink is in dozens of boats. The Olympic Games must be the biggest thing for Croker Oars. 'No, not really,' says John Corbett. 'That's quite a small regatta for us. The Taree regatta is much bigger – there are 110 races a day in that.'

Architectural Models

A warehouse at St Peter's in Sydney is a study in contrasts. A quiet and open space with around a dozen people sitting at computer screens, working with sophisticated design programs; on their desks, alongside the computers, are traditional hand tools – squares and callipers, scalpels, steel rules, paintbrushes of various sizes, pliers and tweezers. The result: houses and high-rise blocks, some aspirationally inhabited – residents in painted-on trendy clothes and shiny shoes, sun lounges on the roof terrace, clocks and modern artwork on the walls – others pale and ghostly, with not a sign of life in sight; office buildings and entire suburbs. All are somehow strangely familiar, a reminder of our childhood, when we spent our days playing in an inconsistently scaled-down world of toy cars and trains, dolls' houses and dolls.

RELIEF AIR FAN
A.C
S

For Modelcraft, however, architectural model making is serious business, an essential early element in the design and building process. The company, set up around 20 years ago and now with offices in Melbourne and Dubai, makes scale models, working off the same plans used to construct the actual buildings. Those models, mainly made in timber or plastic, are commissioned largely by architects or developers, and can be used for anything from presenting a building to council or studying one particular component of a building's façade to encouraging potential buyers into a new urban development or helping the average home owner, who can't read plans, to visualise their renovations. Modelcraft sticks with making just architectural models – other companies around the place make prototypes of virtually anything you can imagine from tape recorders and chairs to landscape designs.

Things were different when Modelcraft started out in Surry Hills in the Eighties. Computers weren't part of life. Half a dozen model makers did everything by hand. 'It was all hand-cut, hand-scored, hand-painted,' says Steve Mosley, one of the company's four directors, who came into the business from the hospitality industry and learnt on the job. 'Virtually everything we do now is computer-generated and computer-cut. It's still assembled by hand and painted by hand, but it's a different world.'

But it's a world that still exists, a surprise to many who predicted it would disappear with the rise of technology and the development of computer-generated images. 'It was worrying at first but computers have ended up helping us.'

Before computer-generated images came along, 'we had to form a mental picture – now something's doing that for us, and they still want the models'. And as a result of the technology, 'we can produce things much finer, more quickly and more accurately than we ever could previously'. In the past a multi-storey building would have taken almost two months to make; these days, it takes about half the time.

And in some ways, says Steve Mosley, computers have helped make the job less labour-intensive and more interesting. 'If you can imagine sticking 200 balconies onto the face of a building and trying to keep them all square and neat and level – the computer can actually provide locators on the balcony and corresponding holes in the façade so they all clip into place. In a way, we produce more kits these days.'

Computers or not, it's still a labour-intensive job, 'and you still need people who are creative, who are good with their hands, skilful, can "three dimensionalise" and are able to put things together, seeing the end result they're working towards, not building blithely'. Many of the people who have worked at Modelcraft over the years have come from related courses or industries – 'everybody from architects not satisfied with architecture, draftspeople, interior designers, industrial designers, and then you'll get the pure hobbyists, the odd rail fanatics and war game enthusiasts'.

No one at Modelcraft has worked out exactly who makes the best model maker. 'It comes down to personality,' says Steve Mosley. 'There are people out there who want to be model makers, but also people who are happy to do it in a transient existence, knowing they're not going to be doing it forever. They're doing it to supplement something else, and in the meantime it's interesting and better than making coffee or waiting on tables.'

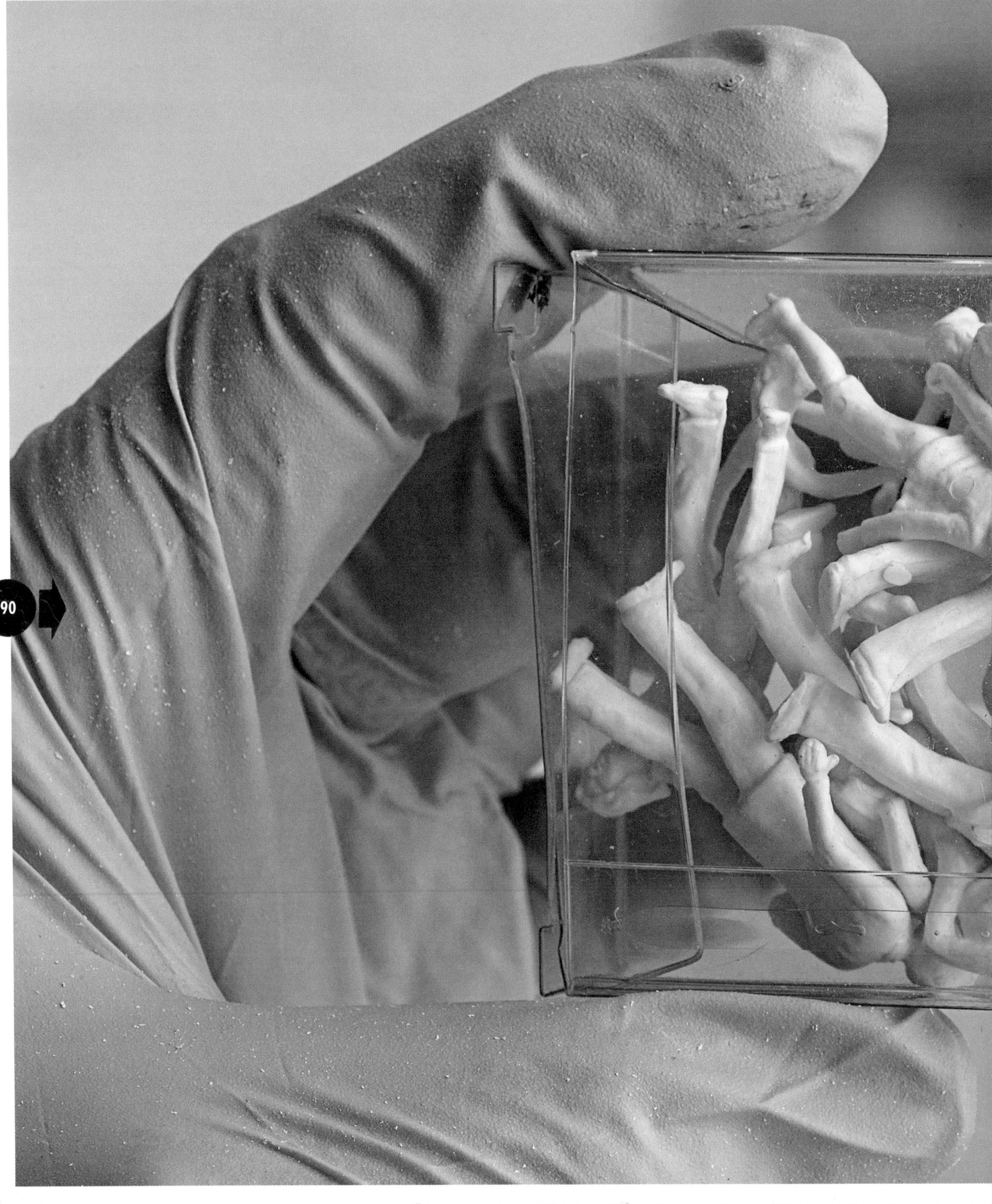

Oddly, some of the least successful model makers are those who loved making models when they were kids. 'They have such a passion for it, and we tend to strip the passion away, because we have more of a business-type approach. It's a shame – they might take weeks and weeks to put something together whereas here it's got to be done in a time frame to a budget. You need to have skills and passion, but not too much passion.'

It's mainly men who make models – there are usually one or two women working at Modelcraft at a time, but Steve Mosley is surprised there aren't more. 'Women are very good model makers, and there should be more of them than men. The work's so delicate, and you've got guys with sausage fingers trying to put together tiny little pieces. Maybe women are smarter and don't want to do it.'

As in all design and building work, some model makers are better at certain aspects than others. 'You get some people who are really quick in digesting information for building the bases of buildings. It's the same with towers, and right down to the roof forms – some put them together really quickly, others struggle with the concept of how they go together. We have people in here who are good at painting, at mixing colours. You can give some people a palette of 10 colours and a couple of hours later they'll have all the colours sorted out. With others, two days later they'll still be having trouble with the first couple of colours. You play to people's strengths.'

Some people work better in timber than plastic; others are more comfortable working in one particular scale. 'There's one guy who does fantastic work at 1:100 scale – it's painstakingly intricate. People like me look at that and think it's my worst nightmare.' Some model makers are like microsurgeons, others more like butchers. The main scales range from 1:25 to 1:500, but can be as large as 1:12 for a study of a portion of a façade, for instance, or as small as 1:2000 for subdivisions. 'The huge small-scale models covering an enormous area are a pain. They're not very challenging, and are more of a technical exercise than anything else. These guys are where the challenge and creative satisfaction come from,' says Steve Mosley, pointing to a partly made 1:100 scale model of a house being made for a development application.

On the day we visited, the model makers were working on five projects – the house, a 1:500 residential tower, a civic model in timber of a library and two 1:100 scale six-storey apartment blocks.

In a year, around 120 models come out of Modelcraft in Sydney. Furniture is made at the workshop, usually the classic pieces – Aalto, Eames, Jacobsen et al, favoured by architects. Paint colours alter depending on the scale, says Steve Mosley. 'If you put realistic colour on a scale model it's going to look wrong. Imagine looking at a building 100 metres away and it looks brown – get closer and the colours become a lot more intense. It's the same with models – the smaller the model the softer the colours should be. Models foreshorten perspective – it's as if they're 100 metres away.'

The one job no one puts their hand up for at Modelcraft, even if they're good at it, is making trees. 'It's tedious,' says Steve Mosley. But every now and then, it has to be done, in a small area away from the rest of the model making. Trees for model making generally come from China and Europe – the European ones mainly come via the model rail industry, as do the models of people. 'Therefore a lot of them carry bags and luggage,' he says. And wear uniforms – railway guards and train drivers, and the odd Stormtrooper, from another type of model series altogether. And come in scales that aren't necessarily quite the same ones as the architects need – N gauge, O gauge, H gauge – and in imperial scale.

The European trees, though, are far more realistic than the Chinese ones. But they're European – spruces and firs and oaks, all in the colours of the forests and woods. The Chinese trees look like mould on sticks and, as the scale gets larger, the colours become harsher, like no leaves ever seen in nature. Sometimes that's fine – the client doesn't necessarily want real-looking trees – the buildings are more important. Sometimes the client is quite happy with a sea of balls on sticks to depict trees – a company in Indonesia can make those more cheaply than Modelcraft itself can.

Modelcraft makes Australian trees and grasses in various scales – Moreton Bay figs, Jackson Bay figs, ghost gums, angophoras, jacarandas, cabbage palms and grass trees. A eucalyptus the height of a hand is sitting on a table – a perfect tiny, grey-hazed replica of a tree found in the bush, its branches as random as those in nature, its trunk convincingly irregular. The art of model making is more apparent here than anywhere else in the studio – there's no plan to this one and, in creating nature, the hand of a human being is both visible and completely invisible.

A supply of tree and landscaping parts is kept in plastic takeaway food containers on shelves in this part of the workshop – tree trunks, of fabric-wrapped wire, look like sticks of incense; sisal used for leaves, kitty litter for gravel, blue metal for boulders, rubber for palm leaves, something that looks like mixed herbs for the forest floor.

They may be boring to make but the Australian trees at Modelcraft give you confidence that computers will never take over altogether; that there will always be architects and designers who want their models to have an element of art to them. Steve Mosley may not have quite so romantic a view. 'The day they bring out holographic models will be the day we cease to function,' he says. But, with the prohibitive cost of such technology, it's a long way off. He doesn't seem the slightest bit concerned.

Bookbinders

96

David Newbold's desk is covered in piles of old books, dozens of tools with wooden handles darkened through time and use, scraps of leather, rolls of gold foil – some imitation and worth $50 a roll, others of 23-carat gold and worth almost $1000 – wooden boxes of brass type. A single-burner electric stove in the corner, designed for cooking – 'It has been known to heat food' – but more commonly used to heat finishing tools for bookbinding. Tools which work like branding irons, to emboss designs and decorative elements into the leather binding of books. He's surrounded by cabinets of type, and rows of shelves of tanners' dyes, some of which are used to dye the Scottish calfskin, the best and finest grain leather he uses in his bookbinding business and, at $1000 for three skins, the most expensive.

In the middle of it all, David Newbold has an old brown leather-bound book, the colour of a Cuban cigar. Its front and back covers – the boards – are in good condition, ornately tooled in decorative panels. The spine, also elaborately decorated, and with the name *Bewick's Quadrupeds* spelt out on it, needs repair. 'The owner wants it repaired, he wants everything kept,' he says. He turns the book to point out the gilding on the edges of the paper. And then as he fans those gilded edges very slightly a bucolic scene appears for a moment. There seem to be rolling lawns and trees, cows, promenading figures, a Greek temple-like structure in the grounds. It vanishes as he closes the book flat. I've never seen anything like it. Has he? 'Oh yes, some people only collect these types of books.'

The difficulty with this particular book, says David Newbold, is that the leather spine is glued to the spine of the book 'and it's weak – as we get a knife under there, it's going to come up in pieces'. He's had the book, published in 1807, in his bookbinders' workshop in the inner Sydney suburb of Glebe for well over a year waiting to get hold of 'a fluid I know about that melts glue – all you do is paint it on, and it draws itself through to the glue, sucks the glue up and you peel it off'. You can't get hold of it in Australia: 'It's highly volatile and might be a little bit carcinogenic.' The more he's tried to find the stuff, the more elusive it's become. The last he heard, it was available in Germany. 'I was led up the garden path, I think I've hit on the binders' myth. It may not exist anymore. It may never have existed.'

And so the owner of the lovely little book has agreed for the spine to be reconstructed. 'We'll take a photo of it, we'll take rubbings and we'll go ahead and do it.' It won't be the original, but in David Newbold's careful hands, it will look as close to the original as anyone could possibly hope for. The leather of the spine will, in colour and grain, match the leather of the boards, its tooling and lettering almost identical to the 1807 workmanship, the whole thing skilfully worked to look as if it could be 200 years old.

David Newbold has been working with books for more than 40 years. He left school at 14, hoping to become a carpenter, but couldn't get an apprenticeship. Having accepted a job as a wood machinist with the NSW Education Department, he was in at the Public Service Board for his last interview, when the man behind the desk took a phone call about bookbinders. David Newbold liked the sound of it, and asked to go and have a look. That afternoon, he decided he wanted to stay in the Government Printing Office. 'It was like it could have been 100 years ago, it really was. There were stacks of account ledgers – massive big books, colourful with indexes cut in at the side, and marbling on the edge. Then there were the law books being bound.'

On his first day, he was taken to a part of the printing works he hadn't seen, 'the machine section, and I was stuck on the machine taking Wyndham System science books off the end – they came off by the ton. We had the one-volume, the two-volume and then they went into chemistry. That set of machinery had been brought in especially for them.'

But it was better than replacing the seats off school chairs, which is what he would have been doing as a wood machinist. And in the second year of his apprenticeship he was sent down to the Mitchell Library where he was surrounded by rare books, and a team of bookbinders willing to share their skills.

David Newbold, who reads history books in his spare time, went back to the Mitchell Library after the end of his apprenticeship and stayed there for 21 years until he started his own bindery, and then set up Newbold & Collins in 1994 with Terry Collins, who had worked in London for many years 'and now lives in Italy'.

There are plenty of bookbinders around, says David Newbold, but most of them are doing machine binding. Throughout his career David Newbold has pretty well only done handwork, and in the old converted stables in a laneway behind Glebe Point Road in inner city Sydney, it's remarkably quiet. The only sound is the radio, with volume dial up no higher than it would be at home. The plug-in single-burner stove and an ancient computer are about the only bits of electrical machinery in the place, 'and there's a gluing machine that gets used every three years when it's a big job'. Old mechanical presses, an 1880s guillotine and hand tools are the main pieces of equipment.

David Newbold goes through the books on his desk and nearby shelves to show what he's working on. 'Someone's collection of Thackeray that was done in a very thin leather – that's been rebacked in a PVC-coated paper which will last. We just can't get the leather that thin anymore.' A 1927 jubilee souvenir book from Manly that was falling apart has been put back together and its paper spine replaced with cloth. A Bible – one of the most common types of book, along with dictionaries, that finds its way into Newbold & Collins – has had its spine replaced, and tattered pages have been

NEWBOLD & COLLINS
DATE 29-6-07
CLIENT
THE Australian Comforts Fund GIFT DIARY 1919
A.C.F.
ALL COMFORTS FREE
(REQUIRED BY)
$220 —

BERT'S
BACKYARD

sandwiched between sheets of fine, transparent tissue paper. Front and back boards have been saved, and so too have the endpapers (the papers inside the front and back covers), along with 'printers' tag and other inscriptions'. There are leather-bound books of poetry and law, a cloth-bound book of English history, bound copies of symphony orchestra programs, and a coverless paperback on the Bolshevik Revolution, which is 'going into a cover – the owner can't find the book anywhere else, it's the best he's been able to get'. For some books, past the point of repair, boxes, designed to stand in bookcases and with spines to look like books, are made to hold the remains.

A shelf is filled with books that people have never been back to collect – a fat copy of Smith's *Mercantile Law* is one that stands out. 'A man asked for them to be bound – he'd had a good win with his lawyer, and it was a present for him. But then he didn't want to know about it – we'd ring him and as soon as he heard who it was on the other end, he'd hang up. I've had three or four of Sydney's top QCs wanting to buy it – in six months' time, once seven years is up, I can sell it.'

A tiny cookbook, *New System of Domestic Cookery*, published in 1839, smaller than a passport and with recipes for such things as pigeon pie, is being taken apart and the sections sewn back together. The bookbinders' needle, slightly bigger than a normal sewing needle to hold the Irish linen thread, is kept in an old wine bottle cork, so it doesn't get lost, on a shelf by David Newbold's desk. It looks as if there's a lot to be done to the book. 'I reckon there's about an hour and a half's work there – it's so small, we've got to be very careful.' He's faster at sewing than I had imagined. A first edition of *1984* is having its dust jacket restored – 'that'll cost a couple of hundred dollars' – and doesn't devalue the book if it's done properly.

Sydney, with its humidity, isn't a great place for books, he says. 'It's not as bad as Brisbane, but not as good as Adelaide. There are books that have been stored there all their lives and there's not much foxing on the paper. Go around Toowoomba or further north into the Tropics and things are bad – I've just done a job where as soon as you bent the paper it snapped.' In a case like that, he says, he'd suggest photocopying the original or looking for a better copy.

He needs a knowledge of bookbinding history, he says, to do his job properly. 'I have to know about the changes in construction and especially the changes in design – fancy going onto a book from 1640 with a tool designed in 1820. You've got to be so aware.' He has the right equipment to work on books dating back as far as 1500, including metal stamps, which are heated to make impressions in the leather, made by an engraver in the Southern Highlands.

Some of the tools David Newbold uses are in cabinets by his desk. Bone 'folders', like oversized paddle pop sticks but each with different shaped ends for varying tasks, are clumped together in one drawer. 'They're an extension of your hand,' says David Newbold, giving an Edward Scissorhands impersonation as he picks up a couple of them. 'They're used to turn the material around, for doing corners, all sorts of things. When I'm putting a new piece of leather on, they'll go in and work like a little lever to move the spine away so I can turn the leather in.' He opens another drawer and pulls out his 'favourite syringe', a lethal-looking metal and glass number, 'for getting down into little places in a book I can't get to – down underneath the leather to lay a bit of glue'. And there are medical scalpels and French paring knives, and old bone-handled butter knives with cut-down blades for separating leather from board, for lifting away one element from another.

Under each workbench in the studio are rolls of cloth in dozens of colours and varying textures, and, rolled in brown paper, animal skins (the blond Scottish calfskin and, from the Sokoto region of northern Nigeria, goatskin, 'naturally tanned there and then coloured in England, no acid goes near it so it lasts and lasts'). From a certain angle, it could be a fabric warehouse. Marble paper – used, among other things, for endpapers and boards, and collected over the years, with some sheets around 100 years old – are kept in low, shallow drawers, which open to a mass of colour, almost too much after the tattered beauty of the old books. Swirls of purple, acid green, intense yellows, and a smoky silver, with marbling reminiscent of the grain of a tree. A good sheet of handmade marble paper can cost $30; a 'machine assisted' sheet, about $8. 'The difference is class – the $8 sheet is the Woolworth's one – it's still marble paper and good for some jobs.'

The biggest job at Newbold & Collins when we visit is the restoration of an original hospital admissions register dating from 1862. It's weeks of work. The leather on the cover is scored, scratched and stained as any workbook would be. Inside, ruled-up columns give patient details – name, age, occupation, religion, length of time in the colony, disease, result. Servant, sawyer, labourer, servant, servant, servant, French

TRACKS JAN-JUNE 1991
TRACKS JAN-JUNE 1990
TRACKS JAN-JUNE 1994
TRACKS JAN-JUNE 1992
TRACKS JAN-JULY 1988
TRACKS JULY-DEC 1997
TRACKS JULY-DEC 1994
TRACKS JULY-DEC 1991
TRACKS JULY-DEC 1990

teacher, digger, the occupation column reads in copperplate. 'Diseases' include needle in foot, rheumatism, fractured finger. The register, says David Newbold, was a mess when it came in, with pages falling out. 'We've taken all the pages down, repaired them, resewn the sections and got it back into its original binding. It's come up better than I'd expected.' A presentation box, with lettering in maroon leather similar to that on the outside of the book, is being made up in the workshop.

It's not only old books that get dealt with at Newbold & Collins. One major part of the business, which keeps one person going three days a week, is in making wedding albums – large format books, which look more like fashion magazines than the traditional photo album, with double-page spread photographs, gatefolds and other layout details more commonly seen in commercial publications. One particular photographer who sends a lot of business Newbold & Collins' way came up with the idea – now copied around the world, apparently – after he'd done a catalogue for a fashion company. 'If people knew the idea had come from a clothing catalogue they'd be shocked,' says David Newbold as he looks through the latest half-made wedding album, with handmade cover, expansive harbourside shots of the bride and groom and detail photos of candles and canapés.

And then there are far less glamorous jobs – the cloth-covered binders for bank statements, the folders for engineering jobs, the covers for restaurant menus, the presentation folders for business pitches. All help keep the company going – not that business has been slow in recent years. As one of the last bookbinders in Sydney to do handwork, Newbold & Collins has been picking up work from other companies closing their doors. Two within walking distance of the Glebe studio have closed in the past three years. In one, the proprietor died at the age of 87; the other had been there since 1939 and the two workmates had made a pledge to stop working if anything happened to either of them. 'Reg was 75 and the old bloke who worked with him was 86 – I'd hit it off with Reg and he rang one day to say Dick wasn't too well and wouldn't be coming back. He said for me to come over and put my name on some of the equipment.' Which he did. And he also got many of his boxes of brass type, some dating back to 1880, at auction when the Government Printing Office closed down. For each typeface, multiple copies of letters and symbols in a number of different sizes – the four-point are virtually impossible to read with the naked eye – fit neatly in rows, separated by wooden blocks, in the old timber boxes. David Newbold pulls out a few more boxes of type, with three of each letter 'right down to Z and then there are three full stops and that's it'. They came from a chain of shoe repair shops which used to put lettering on suitcases. 'They gave up. There are so many fake materials that look real – you put heat to them and they go into holes. They don't give their employees much training time – a day and you're in, and expert at putting heels on stilettos. I'm now known as the letterer of handbags and things, which I don't want to be, but some of the best leathergoods stores around town let people know we're here if they want it.' He doesn't want to be known as a desktop tooler, either, but he's just completed an old desktop as a favour – replacing the leather and tooling a gilded border around the edge. 'I don't want a massive great desk in here – I don't have room.'

Wooden Boats

The one thing people forget about boats is they're potentially lethal, says Llew Sweatman. 'If your car blows up, you can roll to the side of the road…kick the tyres and walk home. If a plank falls off one of these things 300 miles out to sea, the only place it's going is down. Every time you get on board is cause for probable death. You only have to get clonked on the skull and fall overboard, you're drowned. A simple little one-inch plastic bung can be forgotten, and it's goodnight.'

The romance of boating is dashed when Llew Sweatman gets going. It's not a bad thing. He's an instructor at the Wooden Boat Centre in Tasmania; it's reassuring that student boatbuilders are aware they're making more than beautiful objects.

Hull number eight, under construction, is a gorgeous-looking thing, as carefully detailed as a jewellery box and created almost entirely by hand out of huon pine, teak and celery top. The hull itself is painted shiny white, perfectly planed, sanded and painted by hand. A couple of tourists visiting the centre are arguing about it. It's timber coated in fibreglass, says the husband. No, the wife replies. It's layers and layers of paint. She's right.

STN 2 FWD
STN 3
FWD
3
FWD STN
4
FWD STN
5
DWL
WL-1'6"
DWL

The husband's misconception is common, says Llew Sweatman, and is both the best and worst thing anyone can say about one of the centre's wooden boats. 'Quite often the only experience people have had of wooden boats is of beaten-up, planky looking things.' The paintwork on the hull of one of the centre's earlier boats was as ice-smooth as number eight's but the seams between each plank were routed out and made concave, like the belly of a whale.

Hull number eight, the eighth the school has produced, is its name while it's being built. It's 'filthy bad luck' to know its real name until virtually the day it's launched. 'Anything that happens during construction – injuries, mishap, death – is attached to that name. In historical maritime lore there have been boats considered to be unlucky. Some of the stories are apocryphal but I remember there was one ship always having trouble, and when they opened her up to break her up years later they found three of the builders had actually been riveted into the bottom of it and died there.'

Superstition and death seem more appropriate to old boats, not to a new '36-foot motor cruiser built in the Halvorsen style', with a cabin for two, an air-conditioning plant, stereo system and a widescreen TV, but that's the way it is. 'I assume the owner knows the name,' says Llew Sweatman. And someone else at the Wooden Boat Centre may know how many letters the name has, at least, so they know how much room to leave on the stern for it.

A boat like hull number eight takes more than a year to build, with almost all the work carried out by the half dozen or so students who have signed up to see the project from start to finish. It all happens at a workshop on the banks of the Huon River at Franklin, south of Hobart. A workshop clad in vertical timber boards to match the local building style, in a part of the world where varieties of apples you've never heard of are grown, and honesty boxes are left at garden gates.

Inside, the hull takes over most of the workspace, and benches and cabinets around the edge are covered in tools. Tools that carpenters, joiners, cabinet-makers and engineers use. But used in quite a different way: 'Most joiners and cabinet-makers aren't expected to use the fancy planes on anything but the bench, clamped securely in place, not dangled over their knee on a deck or upside down with someone else's shavings dripping into their eyes, while they're trying to get this thing to fit to cigarette-paper standards.'

When we visit, the students are all on the hull, working quietly using hand tools. It's a complex dance with each person doing a specific job, but in tune with everyone else. No one gets in anyone's way.

Among the students at the privately run course is a former butcher, a former landscape gardener. In the past, there have been students who have retired from the corporate world and taken up something they've wanted to do all their lives, and others who, early on, decide they want to spend the rest of their lives sailing around the world. Llew Sweatman himself worked as a field hand in gold exploration and as 'a counter jumper' in a hardware store before doing the course in 2002 and staying on as an instructor. Entry is partly through interview, sometimes by phone. 'We want to find out why they want to come here,' says Llew Sweatman. 'It's fine if it's for a yahoo, as long as it's for a serious yahoo – if someone's not going to be here all the time, there's no point. It disrupts the group.'

The students who can find it toughest, says Llew Sweatman, are engineers – those who are used to working in the 'ordered world of metals and plastics. The trouble with timber is what you do today may not be the same tomorrow. You do something today and it fits perfectly. You put it down on the bench, go away, the temperature changes or the humidity rises and you come back 24 hours later and it no longer fits. It drives them insane.'

Carpenters and cabinet-makers – those who are used to dealing in straight lines, levels and corners – can have trouble too, he says. 'It's a very visual trade. A lot of people can't draw what we would call a fair curve, a nice curve without bumps and wiggles in it.' He talks about 'points in space' between curves for bulkheads, engine boxes, parts of the galley – points you can't measure because they're 'in the middle of nowhere and they're generally not a straight line, and they may or may not be level and may or may not be vertical. The boat is curving in all directions – you can shift three inches and the curve is subtly different. That's where the art and craft of it comes in. If you get it wrong, the boat will be extremely ugly.'

It's not only carpenters and cabinet-makers who may have trouble with such a concept, I think, as I'm talking to Llew Sweatman, trying to imagine points in the middle of nowhere, and yet in the middle of a boat. To be a successful boatbuilder of the type of boat made at the centre, you need to be, he says, 'an engineer, a bridge-

5
AFT STN 5
6
7
DWL

builder, a house builder, cabinet-maker, joiner, 12-volt electrician, blacksmith, painter, jack of all trades, you do all your own glazing, your own plumbing'.

The Wooden Boat Centre used to regularly make small boats – clinker or ply boats – as part of their courses. But a few years ago they discovered 'some students were only interested in small boats and didn't give a toss about big boats, and some the other way around'. They split the courses – six- to eight-week ones for small boats, a year or more for the big boats. However, it's hard to find people willing to commit to the short courses at the same time; the small boats under construction at the centre are built mainly by private individuals, using the space.

But there's a piner's punt there, a flat-bottomed rowing boat made by the school. It's smaller but 'ridgy didge in shape' to a real piner's punt, a type of boat used by loggers on the west coast of Tasmania in the nineteenth century. 'They'd disappear up creeks and rivers for three or four months with all their gear, cut huon pine, roll the logs down towards the river and hope the river flooded and washed the logs down.'

The rivers didn't necessarily flood; the logs didn't always get swept down. Some got lost, or buried in moss and mud, and forgotten about. 'With huon pine, it doesn't matter – you scrape an eighth of an inch off the top and the timber underneath is perfectly good.'

That's the timber the Wooden Boat Centre uses to build its craft – timber that may have been felled by hand by piners now dead for 100 years or more. Huon pine has all the characteristics a boatbuilder wants: 'It's easy to work, extremely durable, it bends easily, steam bends nicely, planes and sands nicely, holds paint nicely, you know it's not going to rot.' Broad sheets of it are stored in piles in the workshop. The forest they came from is still in evidence, and that's to do with more than just the astringent scent of the timber. It comes from the way the timber is cut, not in planks, but 'from bark to bark', from one side of the trunk to the other, to form irregularly shaped pieces, 'curved because most boats are curved'. Each one is numbered, measured and marked up on a list, noting how many curved planks and of what length can be taken from each. 'You try and find mates for each plank – generally when the timber's sawn this way, you're fairly well guaranteed that the next board will give you the partner. If you've got a 14-foot plank on this side of the boat, you'll need a 14-foot one on the other side. You try to get matched pairs all the way through.' Each plank on a boat made at the centre is individual – and all angles are different from plank to plank. 'You can't just cut out a generic shape of plank and bend it round the hull and say that's going to make a boat.'

Boatbuilders like Llew Sweatman carry a pocketful of HB pencils – nothing flash, just the sorts of basic pencils you can buy in a newsagent's. They're hard enough to mark most surfaces and not smear, and 'soft enough not to dig holes in the timber'. They're also hard enough to sharpen to a point, to draw 'a nice fine line'. He points to a line as thin as a fly's leg on a drawing of hull number eight. 'That line represents 1/32 of an inch – if I had a really thick pencil and put a line this thick', drawing a dirty smudge of a line on the page, 'and said it was two inches from there to somewhere else, someone could quite reasonably grab me by the throat and ask is it two inches from this side of the line, or halfway through it or from the other edge. You can't get things to fit when you're looking at a line that's half an inch wide. That's why we need nice little thin pencils – it's hard to split hairs and say I'm on the wrong side of that 1/32 inch of a line.'

Metric measurements are unknown around here – all lengths, as they are traditionally in boatbuilding, are in feet, inches and eighths of an inch – it's an easy system to work with, says Llew Sweatman, especially for the illiterate, as boatbuilders often were in the past.

Computers are rarely used at the Wooden Boat Centre. 'It's a dusty environment, so you'd have some expert coming down here every week to fix them.' The digital camera is about the only high-tech piece of equipment around – photos are taken regularly of the work in progress to send to the boat's owner.

The most traditional methods around are used on each boat. 'It has to have steam frames, so students learn how to do that. It's riveted because that's the best way of doing it, and students have to know how to make copper bolts.' No manufacturer anywhere in the world makes copper bolts in the sizes required for boat building, says Llew Sweatman. He picks up a length of copper rod and demonstrates how it's done, cutting the copper to length and hammering out one end to make its head on an anvil resting on a willow trunk. A thread will be cut into the other end. He gives the head a little pie crust edge 'to make it cute', runs it on the wire wheel to give it a leather grain pattern. The pie crust edge and leather grain pattern are his own marks – signs of his

personality coming through. 'It's a fancy thing I do; if you see a bolt like that on a boat, you can guarantee I've done it, or someone I've taught.'

Each boatbuilder has his or her own way of doing things – the trims around the window of hull number eight, says Llew Sweatman, point to the boat school. Or the extra groove on the edges is someone else's particular detail. He could look at a boat, he says, and know who built it. 'And it sometimes makes all the difference between an ordinary boat and a really nice boat, the amount of massaging and polishing and shaping and tweaking you do.'

Blacksmith

Geoff Barnes is flicking through the photo albums of pieces he's made in the 35 years he's been a blacksmith. Shish kebab skewers, knife racks, candelabra – some quite baronial in design – garden gates, a kitchen dresser, dining tables, cleavers, bird baths, garden benches, woks. 'You can be sucked in by what you can do with cold hard steel once you get it hot and move it around a little bit,' he says. In the forge at the end of the garden, past the pergola, made by Geoff Barnes of steel, and holding up a dripping wisteria, his son Adam is making a crowbar for a friend, another blacksmith 'who prefers arc welding to forging hot steel', to replace one that had been pinched. The crowbar's as tall as his thigh, as thick as a baseball bat; it will be used to prop a gate open. It takes him all morning to make; he could buy one, he says, for about $80 at a hardware store, but there would be no satisfaction in that.

Shoes for the Moscow Circus

Adam Barnes trained at art school, and worked as a potter and stone-carver before joining his father at the blacksmith's forge. He'd been watching him since he was a child, absorbing more information than he could have imagined. 'I'm glad he chose to become a blacksmith,' he says about his father. 'It made it easier for me. Steel's a fairly tactile material, you can do a lot with it. Cut it, change it, bend it, stretch it, make it look organic. I love it.'

Geoff Barnes didn't exactly choose to become a blacksmith. He woke up one morning and thought perhaps he could be one. 'If you like, God called.' He'd had nothing to do with blacksmiths before that – he had a degree in 'biochemistry, physiology, pharmacology and histology' and had trained as a science teacher before being conscripted into the army and sent to Vietnam. He taught for a few months when he got back 'but I was so stressed out I couldn't cope with it'.

The greatest misconception about blacksmiths, he says, and one that he's never had, is that they shoe horses. 'I don't know anything about horses. I don't even know which end to pat, let alone nail a shoe on it. As far as I'm concerned, horses are big dangerous animals with teeth one end to bite you and feet the other end to kick you, so steer clear of them.'

Another misconception, he says, is that it's a dying trade. 'That may have been true after the Second World War, but it's no longer the case. In the Sixties and Seventies there was a great movement in the Western world back to the old handcrafts. Pottery took off, leadlighting and blacksmithing took off. Not so much in Australia maybe, but overseas, in the United States and Europe it certainly did.' But when he talks about South Australian blacksmiths he knows, he has to admit there aren't too many of them, and fewer than there were a number of years ago. 'There aren't many doing the original old-style work that we are. They're mostly doing a lot of modern arc-welded pieces that I don't like very much.'

His first job in the trade, close to where he now lives in Adelaide, was with a firm of agricultural implement makers – 'ploughs and harrows, whatever farmers needed, they made'. He'd answered an ad in the paper for a blacksmith's assistant, 'and they clearly didn't like the look of me but no one else turned up'. In the forge, work was mainly with jigs and dies and presses, with not much done by hand. 'However, the handwork that was done was most impressive – we'd forge bars this big into drilling

rods,' he says, shaping his arms into a circle as round as the circumference of a tree trunk. 'The blacksmith would hang onto the rod with tongs that stood taller than me.' It took two men to lift the tongs, he says.

He lasted at the job for several months, and then discovered ornamental blacksmithing, through a book on contemporary ironwork by a German blacksmith. He started collecting tools, and built the shed he works out of now. It's in the back of what was, at the time, his grandparents' house. 'They let me set up here, which was very kind of them, I could never have afforded to lease premises.'

There aren't any other obvious signs of industrial activity on the street; one neighbour objected when the forge was set up, saying it was a residential area. Geoff Barnes asked why the neighbour didn't mind someone else having a furniture business a few doors away. 'He said he supported him because he was a Second World War veteran. I asked him how come he didn't support veterans from other wars. He was all right after that.'

He'd learnt some of the basics of blacksmithing at the agricultural implement makers, and also went to night school, where he ended up teaching on and off for 27 years. 'In the end I would have taught hundreds of people – most doing it as a hobby. Only about three or four that I can think of became blacksmiths.'

Geoff Barnes' forge takes up as much room on the suburban block as his house, and is packed with blacksmithing tools and equipment; steel rods and scrap metal, including old springs; a coke-burning fire in the centre. Strung along a beam are pieces made by blacksmiths years ago – plumbers' tools, spanners, bootscrapers, a dingo trap. He's never been asked to make a trap himself, he says, but has made cattle brands.

The fire in the forge is set every morning, with coke stored in 44-gallon drums and bought half a tonne at a time. You don't see smoke coming from the chimney; no one would know there was a fire going inside.

'It can idle all day on two shovelfuls of coke,' says Geoff Barnes. 'It doesn't chew up much.' It's only when air's sent through the flames, via a fan under the floor, that the coke burns quickly, as the temperature heats up to thousands of degrees Celsius, enough to turn the steel as soft as liquorice. Or even burn it. He shows us a rod that's useless – heated for too long, it's distorted and dull. 'If I'd left it longer, it would have burnt into two halves,' he says. 'It turns into grey muck.' He picks up a few grey flakes from the ground. When he's working it, Geoff Barnes gauges the temperature of the steel by its colour. 'If your colour's too dull a red, it's too stiff to work.'

He gets burnt about once a year, he reckons, 'picking up the wrong end of a bar I've forgotten to cool down, but you learn pretty quickly to get out of the way of things'. His hands are tough from handling hot steel. 'I don't wear gloves – it lacks a certain control if I do, it feels a bit muffled.' ABC Radio National plays in the forge: 'It's my only way of keeping in touch with the world.' Not that he listens while he's actually working. 'You can't let your mind wander because pretty soon you'll find the steel will wander too.'

Blacksmithing was once 'the king of the trades which every other trade needed because we made the tools', says Geoff Barnes. But then it became 'the most despised and lowest trade. I can't understand why. It required an enormous amount of skill, but was seen as dirty. Fitting and machining and boilermaking had gleaming, high-tech equipment – they were seen as much more glamorous.' Blacksmiths used to be the only tradesmen who could cut up steel – they'd heat it up 'and give it an almighty whack with a hammer', but now there are 'abrasive cut-off saws, power hacksaws, oxy torches…so many modern ways of cutting up steel, you no longer have to worry about the old low-tech way'.

But blacksmiths are still the ones who make many of the tools. Geoff Barnes has collected a number of his tools from junk shops or from abandoned forges, long forgotten in weed-ridden yards behind factories and workshops, but has to, at times, fabricate the right tool for a particular job. When dealing with red-hot steel, you want a pair of tongs that will grip it firmly, not let it wobble, or flick about when struck with a hammer. Geoff Barnes points to a rack of around 30 pairs of tongs. 'And there are another 50 over there, of all shapes and sizes.' With various shaped jaws, and handles at differing angles, to match the section being worked on. There are dozens of each tool – at least 50 hammers – 'hard ones, soft ones, different-shaped ones, heavy ones, light ones, depending on the job you're doing'. Some are covered in dust, perhaps not used for 20 years; on others, the face has worn away until it's gleamingly smooth.

Geoff Barnes has made tools for lettering – he only needs three to do the whole alphabet. One straight, one slightly curved, one very curved. 'I don't know how I worked that out – you look at the job and think about how to break the letters down in the simplest way.' It's the same with any job he does – he has to break it down into parts, and work out the order to do it. An amateur, he says, will put the curve or bend in first, 'but then, as you can imagine, the bar becomes very unmanageable and wants to flop down in the direction of the curve'. Any bends, he says, are the last things to do. His science training didn't help at all when it came to working out the logic of blacksmithing, he says. 'If anything helped me, it was being given a Meccano set as a child. It teaches you how mechanical things go together, how things can be made to work and interact.'

Like most trades, blacksmithing has a language all its own. Geoff Barnes talks about the hardy and the hardy hole; he talks about bottom fullers and top fullers, bottom swages and top swages, all tools to help cut, shape and put marks into the metal. 'Then there are flatters, which, as you can guess, are for flattening or smoothing material, and a variety of punches for punching holes. After that, they don't have names – they're just tools.'

It takes two to do much of a blacksmith's work – one to hold the steel in place, the other to wield a hammer. Geoff and Adam Barnes work together on various parts of the crowbar, as they shape and flatten the metal. They work methodically; Adam Barnes holds the hot bar down on a flatter. 'Hit,' he shouts, when he's ready. Geoff

Barnes whacks down with a hammer. Adam Barnes adjusts the bar slightly. 'Hit.' This goes on for about five minutes, the metal staying hot long enough to be worked. The end narrows down, into a recognisably crowbar shape.

When Geoff Barnes is designing a piece, he draws it up full size in chalk on a steel bench, and as he's working 'I bring the bar over and check directly with the drawings. The advantage of a steel bench over paper is it's not going to burn when I put hot steel on it.' Gates, candleholders, fire tools, grates, 'everything that had to be done to a particular size would have been done on the bench. Even the simplest job would be laid out on the bench if it involved any hot work at all. I need a visual picture of the finished size so I can work out which piece of the bar to start off with.' Geoff Barnes should have made a habit of standing up on the bench to take a photo of each job so he had a record of his designs, he says. 'But once something's done, I'm onto the next.' A lifetime of work is embedded in that chalk-dusted steel bench, expanding and contracting as it comes into contact with hot steel.

Cricket Balls

The Platypus Sporting Goods sign on the outside factory wall is peeling, coming off in great flaps. It's the first factory we've been to that genuinely looks as if it's been there for more than half a century. It's strangely exciting to see something so much part of a different time – beautiful in its own way.

Platypus was set up by Dave Brown in Melbourne in the Depression after he'd been sacked from his job at another cricket ball company for having chicken pox. 'That's what happened in those days – there wasn't sick pay, so if you didn't turn up for work, you didn't have a job,' says his grandson Gary who works at the factory now, mainly concentrating on the accounting side. Gary's wife, Robyn, works at Platypus too, so does his brother Rodney, 'who's good with his hands' and looks after the production side of the business, and his son Adrian and nephew, also called Dave. All of them go on holiday to watch cricket, or go off to the MCG between Christmas and New Year for the Test Match. Adrian's eight-year-old son worked in the factory, too, during a recent school holiday to earn money to buy a Game Boy. Most of the girls in the extended family have found other things to do. 'We didn't encourage the boys,' says Gary of his son and nephew. 'But the opportunities came up and they wanted to work here.' A couple of other men work at Platypus too – they're not part of the family, but have been there for 30 years or more.

It turns out the sign out the front is just a bad paint job (or a very good paint job, depending on your foolishly romantic view of life). 'Did you see the cricket ball sign on the corner of the building – that was painted at the same time and that's all right.' The factory has only been in the present building since about 1990 – before that it was across the road, or down in Northcote or in the backyard of Dave Brown's house.

The Platypus factory, a former golf bag factory, is as crumblingly beautiful inside as out – rough timber floors, opaque windows, high ceilings and hanging fluorescents, mysterious machines that could have been designed by Heath Robinson (but were in fact invented by Gary and Rodney's father), unruly piles of boxes, each containing a dozen shiny Jaffa-like cricket balls, letters painted directly onto the brick wall at one end of the work area spelling out in two different typefaces 'T-H-I-N-K QUALITY'.

Platypus is one of the last cricket ball companies in Australia. There used to be dozens of them, mainly one-man operations and each making balls for local teams and clubs. Now, Platypus sells 100,000 balls a year 'to wherever cricket's played' but mainly to the drier places; not many go to England 'because the balls have a totally different finish over there for the wet ground'. The lacquer on an Australian ball is quite tough for our drought conditions, whereas the English ones have an oil finish.

Platypus balls can be found in matches 'from Saturday afternoon cricket right up to district premier cricket' – everywhere except Test and Shield level, of which the company's only Australian opposition, Kookaburra, has the monopoly. 'They've got the approval and that's it,' says Gary Brown. 'They've been using them for years and don't want to change. It's something I've never been able to understand; the AFL will approve five balls, charge each company a lot of money and then use the one they want. That's money for jam, but they don't do that in cricket. There's no rhyme or reason for it.'

When Dave Brown started Platypus in the Thirties, his wife, who'd never had a thing to do with cricket balls beforehand, used to machine-stitch them on her Singer sewing machine in the living room. 'I don't know how she did it,' says Gary Brown. 'The leather's that hard, but I suppose the machines were quite sturdy in those days.' Nowadays, four rows of stitching around the middle of the Platypus cricket balls are done by an industrial machine in the East Preston factory, using linen thread, with the last two rows (one on each side), which hold the halves of the ball together, done by hand in a factory in China. Until 10 years ago they were hand-stitched here, but the combination of an increase in RSI, with associated workers' compensation issues, and a decrease in the number of people prepared to do manual labour made going offshore the only practical possibility. Every couple of months, 18,000 balls are sent to the shoe factory for finishing – about 1000 workers are making shoes 'and we've got 12 in a corner just doing the cricket balls'.

A lot of hand-stitching is done in India, but Gary Brown sees an advantage to getting it done in a country that knows nothing about cricket. 'The Indians have been making cricket balls for centuries, and do it their way, with hand-stitching for all rows – we wanted to make them our way.'

Every now and then Platypus needs a few extra balls in a hurry – there's no time to wait for them to come back from China. Shane Taylor, who has worked at the factory for more than 30 years, sits down at a saddle-like stool and stitches a couple of dozen. He shows us how it's done, with the halves of the ball, the colour of sealing wax, clamped together in a gadget that looks like a nutcracker. He has a needle and thread in one hand, needle and thread plus awl in the other. The awl works ahead of the needles, scooping through and making holes in each side of the ball, as the needles cross from one side to the other to bind the halves together. The action is swift and rhythmically hypnotic, and it's difficult to tell the difference between the hand-stitched and machine-stitched rows.

The beauty of hand-stitching over machine-stitching, says Shane Taylor, is that an expert stitcher can adjust the tension of the thread depending on the varying thickness of the leather to leave a perfectly smooth join – a machine can't feel those subtle differences. It took him a day to learn hand-stitching, a couple of months to get up to speed. The first day he made about six balls; after a couple of months he

PLATYPUS
PLATYPUS

could make 38 in a shift. Both men and women, often new immigrants, did the hand-stitching; at its peak, there were about 10 working full-time on the balls. In the last few years before Platypus finished stitching, a number of Chinese people worked on it in the factory. 'They took it on well,' says Gary Brown. 'That's another reason we looked to China for the finalisation of the ball.'

Shane Taylor doesn't like cricket. 'Can't stand it, hate it,' he says when I ask him about it. I'm not surprised – he looks as if he'd be more into motorbikes, which he is, than cricket. He'd made footballs for a couple of years at another Melbourne factory – 'It was just a job, I knocked at the door and that was it' – and it was only when that closed down that he moved to Platypus. He could make a cricket ball from start to finish if he had to. He's made other types of balls. For a while, the factory made hockey balls – 'basically a white cricket ball', according to Gary Brown – softballs and baseballs, but now they're almost all made in China.

It's hard to imagine a more complicated sporting ball than a cricket ball. For a start, there are far more different types than I knew existed. Different weights, different materials, different quality leather, some plastic (and even these are hand-stitched), different colours (for night and 20-20 cricket and for kids who aren't so serious about the game), and then some made with four pieces of leather rather than two. The four-piece balls are better quality than the two: 'A good bowler can use a four-piece better than a bad bowler – a two-piece will automatically swing, whereas you have to work with a four-piece.' In an office at Platypus, there's a cricket ball with a great chunk taken out of it so you can see what's inside – layers and layers of stuff, just like the inside of the Earth.

It starts with the outside of the ball – the leather, alum-tanned and dyed just up the road at a tannery in Northcote, then cut at the factory into rounds or half circles (rump for the top-quality balls, shoulder and belly for the lower grades), graded for thickness in a mysterious machine (if you were offered a million dollars to guess what it was for, you'd come away empty-handed), hot-moulded into shape and trimmed to size. The trimmed-off circles of leather, several picked up from the factory floor, are just the right size for bracelets.

In the middle of the ball is a cork and rubber core – the granulated raw material is stored in a wooden trough and looks like horse feed. The cork comes from Portugal, the rubber from recycled tyres. There's an old tin scoop in the trough to measure it

out – even more like something for a horse. The mixture is weighed, down to the last hundredth of a gram, before it's put into a spherical mould and baked in the oven to make it nice and solid, but not too hard that it would hurt the bat. There's a timer so it doesn't burn, but Shane Taylor reckons he can tell by the smell of it when it's done. And then he has a contraption for trimming the cooked cork to make a perfect sphere out of it – a contraption that was put together years ago, but modified by Shane Taylor with a length of metal he found in the 'pile in the corner' and a tennis ball around the handle to make it more comfortable to use.

Depending on the quality of the cricket ball, the core is wrapped in a number of layers of cork sheeting, which look like inner soles of shoes, and bound in place by machine to just the right tension with wet woollen yarn, the type you'd use for knitting. Wet so that as it dries, it tightens around the layers to give the ball the right amount of bounce. I ask Shane Taylor what he thinks about as he sits at the various machines. 'Fishing,' he says.

There's a special oven, too, for the wool drying. No timer for this one. 'It's up here,' says Shane Taylor, as he taps his head. He can tell by the 'weird smell' when the wool's at the point of going from being dry to being overcooked. He takes a batch out and sticks them under my nose. 'See what I mean.' It would take me more than a few hours in the Platypus factory to master the art of wool sniffing. It doesn't help that also in the oven is a foil-covered baking dish, heating up the meat pies for Friday lunch. 'Oh yes, there's often food in there,' he says. 'Lasagne sometimes.'

The half-made, wool-wrapped balls are as colourful as Christmas decorations. Royal blue, tan, yellow, purple; you wouldn't know there was anything else inside, they just look like balls of wool at this stage. They seem colour-coded, perhaps royal blue for top quality, tan for the junior balls. But there's no logic to it – the woollen mills (there are a few still left in Australia) sell off the ends of runs, and the colours that no one wants. In a game as complex as cricket, there's something fitting about the possibility of a baby pink core in a high-ranking ball.

After the corked and wool-wrapped cores come back from being encased in leather in China, they're branded in gold, mainly with the regular Platypus logo and specifications. But as in the old days, Platypus also sells to individual clubs, some of which buy 20 dozen balls a month – Yarra Valley Cricket Association, Cricket Albury Wodonga, Mornington Peninsula Cricket Association, among others. All have their individual brass stamps, each quite different, all sitting together in a drawer. Under heat – it used to be bare flame before the days of occupational health and safety – two heavy brass stamps reach branding temperature and are clamped against each side of a ball. Within minutes, a brand new and a very old ball is finished.

Hat Blocks

Doug Osborne is one of the few people in Australia who makes hat blocks for a living. He has more than 300 milliners from around the country on his books; orders are starting to come in from Europe and the United States. When I ring some of the top milliners in Melbourne to find out who makes their hat blocks, they point me towards Doug Osborne, who works out of his garage on the way to Bendigo.

Doug Osborne wears hats. Not all the time. 'Top hats, trilbies, they're fun hats for me. I can come across a beautiful thing made by a milliner, or have a hat made from one of my blocks. It's displaying my wares, if you like.' And he has a very organised filing cabinet. It's in a little office behind his garage. Folders, neatly lined up, with tags saying things like cocktails, coolies, doughnuts, satellites, buttons, cartwheels, diors, berets, caps. Only the last two give any indication of being types of hats. Open a folder and there are faxes of rough sketches, some not showing the slightest artistic talent,

and pictures of hats photocopied so many times they're barely visible; torn-out photos from the social pages or overseas fashion magazines, shots of celebrities, all wearing hats – often with a note attached, 'I want one of those but a bit bigger, a bit deeper, a bit whatever'; the odd well-drawn and detailed fashion illustration, measurements and various angles included. All orders from milliners for hat blocks. All two-dimensional images that Doug Osborne has to interpret into three dimensions. Very occasionally he'll be sent a full-scale model of a hat, made of Chux dishcloths stiffened with glue, as a guide for a hat block.

From these strange and diverse pieces of raw material, Doug Osborne will start building up a picture of how he imagines the milliner wants the hat to look. He has to imagine what the hat looks like from the back, from the other side. The milliner may have a completely different image in her mind. When Doug Osborne talks about milliners, he uses the feminine pronoun.

He'll make working drawings of the hat design and from that comes the hat block. One time he spent an hour and a half with a milliner. 'I'm a reasonable artist, relatively. We arrived at a design, probably had 15 drawings, upside down, inside out, back to front. I made the block perfectly to the drawing that we'd agreed on and she came in and said, "That's so bulk ugly, I hate it."' There was no way, she said, that it could be modified. He stuck it on the shelf and started again. 'A week later another milliner came into the workshop and said that's gorgeous, and bought it.'

Doug Osborne's garage workshop looks like any serious woodworker's workshop. Planks of wood in the corner. A wall of carpenter's tools – hammers, chisels, screwdrivers, saws and axes. A lathe, an angle grinder, a band saw 'which could cut your hand off in one easy sweep', a planer, benches and shelves of tools and partly finished work, a soft carpet of sawdust.

A box of hat blocks from a college have come in for repair. Some have chunks chopped off or deep knife marks around the base; others are chipped or look gnawed; they're all full of pin holes. 'It's amazing how long they'll struggle on with them.'

He hasn't always been making hat blocks – his first was in about 2000 when Louise Macdonald, one of the country's top milliners, asked him to (a friend of his, Ann, was taking hat-making classes with her). 'It worked and looked good. I can't remember how long it took – probably an awful lot of time, but I thought it was brilliant.'

And so, when many other men are thinking about golf and fishing, Doug Osborne, who's in his late sixties, started a new career. It's not the first time that's happened. When he left school in England, he'd wanted to go into the army but was a year too young. 'I couldn't hang around, so started an engineering cadetship, designing car bodies, and worked in that for nine years.' After the bottom fell out of the British motoring industry, he went into medical engineering, 'making anaesthetic equipment, special-purpose surgical equipment, bits of weird and wonderful things'. His boss there had started the company 'which grew to be the best in England' after being sacked as incompetent as a laboratory technician at the age of 56. 'He was a brilliant inventor, such a lateral thinker. I was a book learner, had a couple of degrees in engineering, but he knew a damn sight more than I could ever learn. He took on jobs other people said couldn't be done – I think that stirred me.'

He was driving home from work one evening, 'it had taken me an hour to do 10 miles, and had been raining for three weeks.' It was the Sixties, and Doug Osborne and his family joined the wave of 10-pound Poms. He worked as an engineer for a while in Victoria, 'but had some furious rows with the managing director, told him where he could stick his job and have never done a day's work in engineering since'. After that, he says, he lived off his wits. One job involved helping chiropractors with their business – he ended up becoming a chiropractor in 1979, and still sees a few patients.

No one taught him to make hat blocks – he did spend a day with an old block-maker, but he'd already been in the business for a year or two by then. He offered to work 'for free for a year with one of the block-makers in the UK, but just got utter rejection from him, he didn't want to let anyone know his craft'. Doug Osborne would be prepared to share his craft with anybody. 'I get pleasure in teaching people.' So far, no one seems to be interested.

When he started, he assumed there were only a few basic hat-block shapes, planned to make models of each and then 'knock them out on a copy lathe'. It doesn't work that way. 'Every milliner wants something different.' The blocks, he says, are not designed to be perfect replicas of hats, but guides for milliners to work with. He doesn't have hat blocks sitting around in his workshop for long – they're made to order, some from standard designs, and leave as soon as he finishes them. Except for one – with a great big built-in bow carved into the front. 'That's the way she wanted it, instead of making the bow separately and sticking it onto the finished hat. Sometimes milliners ask for ridiculous things and you say it won't work, but make it anyway. It didn't work. That's there to remind me not to do it again.'

Once he's drawn up the design for a block, 'I have to work out how to make it. Sometimes I'll scratch my head for hours, but eventually sort something out.' Most hat blocks are in one piece; others, in which the crown is broader at the top than the base, need to be made in several interlocking pieces, like a child's wooden puzzle, that can be dismantled to allow the finished hat off. They're all made of jelutong, available from a couple of timber yards in Melbourne, a 'gorgeous wood to work with because it doesn't have knots in it and the milliners like it because they can stick pins in it'.

All except the flattest hats have finger holes in the base, like a bowling ball, but set in at an angle – 'one of Doug's inventions' – so the milliner can get a good grip as she works. And for all but the flattest hats, he'll need to glue a few planks together; and form a basic shape on the lathe if he can, otherwise he'll work it by hand. Following the drawings 'but I'm never going to copy exactly what's there, I'm not Michelangelo',

he'll carve and sculpt the timber, using a combination of tools, some of which are his own inventions. Like the rolling pins, of various diameters – some left as they are, others slightly modified – and vase-shaped blocks made on the lathe, all of which are painted with glue and rolled in grit to become sanding blocks, each one designed to create a specific shape. Some hat blocks – a simple cloche or pillbox – may take only 20 minutes to make; others up to 20 hours. He pulls out a picture of something that looks like a timber tadpole. 'It's not economical to make, but the creative pleasure is worth it.' He doesn't think it's a particularly good hat, though, he says.

A hat block for a fedora is sitting on the bench. From it, more than any of the others, you can imagine the end result, in felt. It's a surprise to see the dent in the side which, in the finished hat, always looks so rakishly spontaneous.

Doug Osborne's hat blocks are untreated – pale as balsa and perfectly smooth. 'The milliners I talk to say it's a waste of time to do anything more. It's a mould to make something else on; if it was the finished article I'd love to finish it off. My friend Ann's aunt was a milliner for 50 years and her blocks are still untreated, unpolished and still as good as gold 100 years on.'

Shearers' Pants

I rang a bloke one Friday afternoon because I'd heard he made pretty good shearers' pants and shirts. Friday afternoon wasn't a good time to call.

He told me he couldn't care less if his business closed down, he was almost 80, and with mulesing and everything else, things were bad in the shearing industry. He didn't want any more customers and he couldn't help me, he said.

I told him I couldn't care less either if his business closed down but I wanted to do a story about him.

He asked me who the patron saints of various countries were. I got them right.

'You're cleverer than you think you are, aren't you.'

He told me he'd had a load of shearers in that day, and he'd had 30 beers. 'I usually have 42 beers but my doctor told me to cut down seeing I'm nearly 80.'

'I'll phone you back when you haven't had 30 beers. When would that be?'

'Six-thirty on a Sunday morning.'

I asked him if I could drop in and see him sometime. 'You'd be wasting your time, I'm never here. I'm in and out like a fiddler's elbow.'

He was telling me how ugly the Sydney Harbour Bridge and the Opera House were and how the world would be better if they were knocked down and asked me if I knitted and then said he had to get on with stuff. He took my phone number.

The next Monday I had a call from a bloke who said he'd found my phone number on his desk and had no idea what it was doing there and had no recollection of talking to me. I told him what I wanted again.

No, he said, I wouldn't want to do that. I don't need publicity. I had something in the paper once and I got four phone calls from secretaries of big businessmen saying their bosses had told them to ring me up and say they had to have my catalogue. I told them to tell their bosses that they didn't have to have my catalogue.

I told him that he'd asked me who the patron saints of various countries were.

'Did I – that's what happens when I get on the musical milk.'

He told me again he didn't need more business and how he was useless on his computer and sending out an invoice took 14 keystrokes and he'd get up to 13 and make a mistake and have to start again.

'You're one up on me,' I said. 'I'm still writing out my invoices by hand.'

We talked a bit longer until he pressed the wrong button on the phone and it turned into a fax machine. He rang me back five minutes later and said would I mind if he had a bit more of a think about being in the book.

Take as long as you like, I said. It must be a bit odd having someone ringing you out of the blue and asking if they can write about you for a book.

Not as odd as someone saying to you they don't want to be in it.

I hadn't heard from the shearers' pants man for a few weeks. I rang him. He sounded terrible. I told him who I was again and that I wanted him in my book.

'I don't reckon I'll be anywhere much longer,' he said. 'I'm nearly 80 years old – I haven't got Alzheimer's, I always said I had juvenilia – but this is something different.'

'How do you feel with juvenilia?'

'Young and stupid.'

'You sound pretty bad now.'

'I went drinking with some blokes from the Murray. I must have picked up the flu from them. I've been using the hangover cure all my life but I can't do that now.'

He told me about his doctor not believing he could drink 42 beers. 'I used to make clickers to count sheep, so the doctor and I went out on the piss one night and he went click, click, click for each beer. Then we went back to his place and had a bottle of whisky.' The doctor had clicked 85 beers before the whisky.

'That's all over now, blokes standing round mulga logs watching them turn to ash and telling tales of rural Homer. They don't do that anymore.'

'You're sounding better already.'

'I wasn't bunging it on before, but I have a very sick way of answering the phone when I see it's a local call. None of the shearers call from a local number. I know it'll be someone I don't want to talk to. I'll say "Do you know me?" and they'll say no, and I'll say to them, "Didn't your mother ever tell you not to talk to strangers?" Or someone from the House With No Steps. What a stupid idea building a house with no steps. Look, I really am sick – why don't you ring me back in two weeks' time and

I don't want you to mention my name or where I am or the trousers, but I'll tell you a very interesting story about footwear.'

'Is that you, George?'

'No, it's not, it's Leta Keens, the one writing a book. You said to ring you back in a couple of weeks.'

'Friday's not a good day for me. Ring me back another time.'

'What day's good for you, and God, you sound better than you did last time.'

'Tuesday, and by Christ I was crook. Bad dose of flu, got into the lungs. I'm never obese but I turned into a skeleton.'

'Oh dear.'

'It's all right, darling, it's just that I'm aged. I've lived a good life. If I dropped dead tomorrow the only regret I'd have is that I'd miss your phone call on Tuesday.'

Dance Shoes

I first came across Salvio's years ago at a fiesta at a flamenco studio at the top of an old flour mill in Newtown. The dancing was intense, the dancers feisty and the singing strangely foreign but it was the shoes that made the most impression. Old-fashioned like something from a faded photograph. Some black, some the colour of blood. Blocky heels, narrow straps, toes that would never be seen in a shoe shop. I had to have a pair.

Most, it turns out, were made at Salvio's which, in a suburban strip between a fish and chip shop and a chemist and opposite the Randwick Ritz cinema, doesn't make its presence felt loudly. People on their way to see a film have, apparently, walked past it for years and not noticed it. There's no permanently open door on the glass-fronted store. The window display of ballet flats, ballroom sandals and jazz shoes on metal shelves is lacklustre. The well-worn sign – Salvio's Ballet & Toe Shoes – on the upstairs window must have been painted as soon as the family company moved in, in 1944.

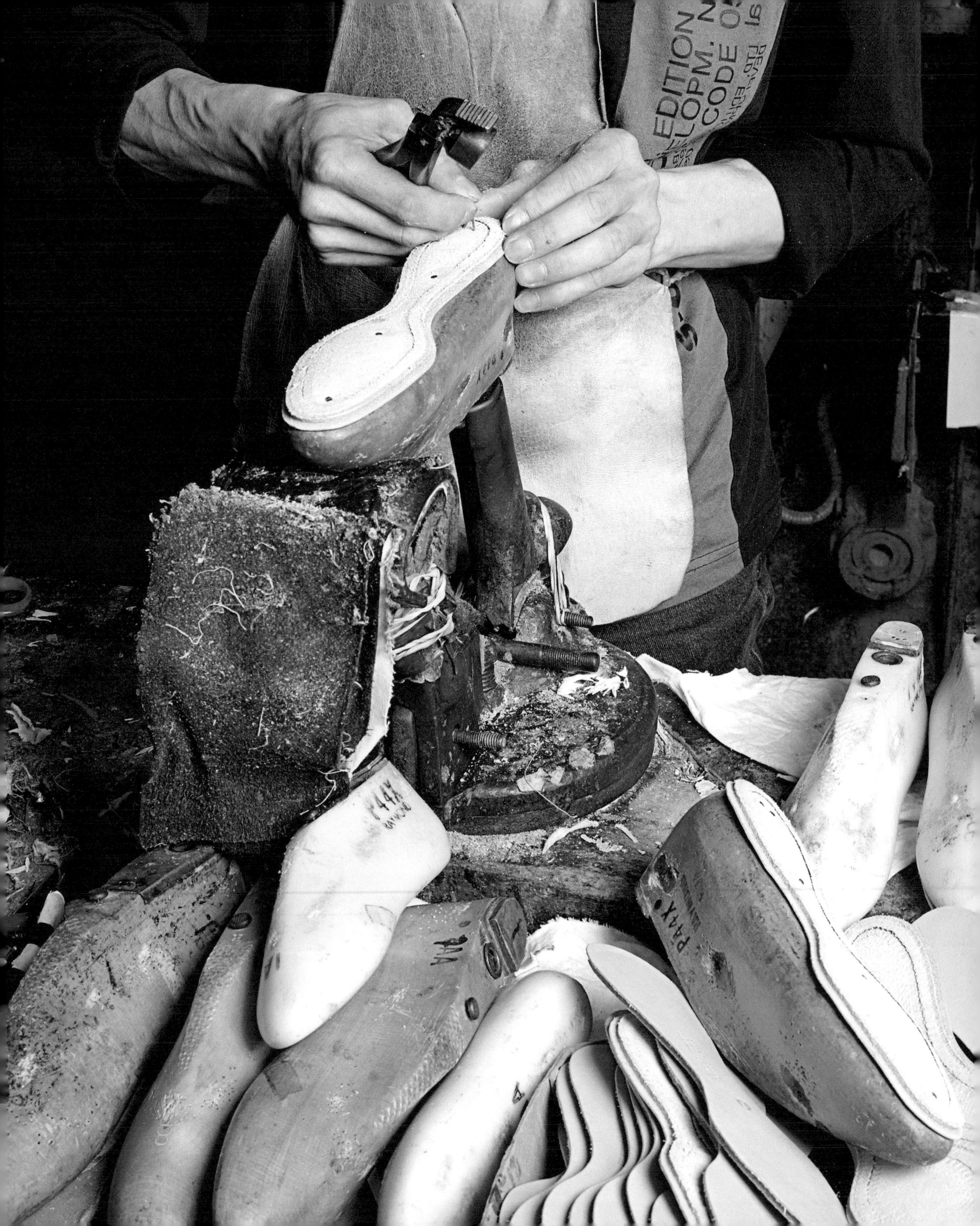

By 1944, Salvio's, the dance-shoe maker, had been going for more than 60 years. It started when Enrico, who was born in Capri and was to become the first of the Australian branch of the Salvio family, stepped off the boat in Melbourne in 1881 and set up his manufacturing business. His grandson Ted is 'all a bit vague' about what brought Enrico, in his early twenties, here. He doesn't know either whether he came from a shoemaking family. 'I think he came out on his own, but I'm not sure – we did go over to Capri once and were going to see where he'd lived and find out about him but it was a public holiday and we didn't see anything.'

In a file at the shop, he's still got his grandfather's original travel document – no photo on it, but descriptions of his nose, his forehead, his eyes – but it's too dog-eared and worn and stuck together with sellotape to read. And Ted's father, Harold Francis Salvio, a betting man and also involved in the family business, had jotted down a few racing notes on it. Those are clear enough. In the file, there's also a photo of Harold, taken in 1936, kneeling at the feet of dancer Tamara Tchinarova as she tries on a pair of pointe shoes. She was on tour with the Monte Carlo Russian Ballet, and later moved here and married actor Peter Finch. Hair pulled back and over her ears like a swimming cap, toes pointed, ribbons dangling, bentwood chair in the background. Harold slick in a three-piece suit and tie, shoes shining, both of them looking intently at his work.

Enrico eventually moved up to Sydney and worked out of a building in Darlinghurst for years before shifting with Harold to the upstairs section of the building Salvio's is in now, close to where the family lived. It had been a pool hall before they moved in. Downstairs on one side was a hairdresser, barber on the other. From the sounds of it, the men in the barber's spent more time smoking and talking than anything – the walls of the shop were so nicotine-stained they couldn't be scrubbed clean, and, once Salvio's shop moved downstairs, wallpaper had to be used to cover the filth.

Upstairs, up the stairs worn down by millions of footsteps, would have looked much the same in the Forties as it does today. Walls lined with lasts – then they were all tea tree, now they're mainly plastic, which is much tougher and easier to work with and, from a distance, looks like the real thing to an outsider. Stacks of heels ready to be encased in leather. A metal drying stand for soles that looks like a cage for a pair of eagles. A couple of industrial stitching machines, one of which is almost as old as the company, and looks quite clinical, something you'd find in a hospital. Rolls of leather in all colours, and even the odd pattern – harlequin stripes or tiger skin. In the old days, the leather came from one of the tanneries in nearby Botany, 'but they all closed down – with the pollution laws, they wouldn't be allowed to do a lot of what they used to do then'. Now Salvio's buys a lot of its leather from Toowoomba Saddlery.

Rows and rows of half-made thigh-high boots, minus soles, are lined up on shelves, ordered for a show on a cruise ship. A couple of men are sitting at benches and, with old timber-handled hand tools and brushes, pleat and fold and glue satin ballet slippers or leather uppers to soles. Their fingers work quickly and lightly. Others tap tacks into leather with wooden-handled mallets. Or sit at a bulky machine, near the front window, punching out leather shapes, constantly angling the material, like you do with pastry, to waste as little as possible. And any leather that's not popular anymore – the harlequin stripe or the orange tiger skin – is used for inner soles; this is a business where everything gets used. Downstairs, on a draining board, old Vegemite and gherkin jars are full of dye; samples of coloured leather and bindings are stuck to the kitchen cabinets, with notes to say which blends have been used. A microwave oven is used to heat the dyes.

Everyone who's ever worked here has been trained by Ted, who left school at 15 to start in the factory – 'I wasn't given any option and can't imagine doing anything else' – or by his father or grandfather. 'We've had people who've been in the trade come in, and breaking their habits is harder than starting with someone who's never done a thing before,' says Ted. 'Somebody who's been doing it for 30 years their way, you've got buckley's of changing them. All you need to be is good with your hands and then you can teach them.' You can usually pick it straightaway, he says. 'Give them a simple job of gluing soles and there'll be more glue on their hands than on the soles, so "sorry, bye bye".' For those who do stick it out, it usually ends up a job for life.

When Salvio's first opened in Randwick, shoes were sold from a small alcove upstairs. 'We'd have people queuing up the stairs,' says Ted, who used to spend four or five evenings a week at dances in town halls in Randwick, Petersham, Marrickville and Rockdale. There were about 20 dance schools in the area then and, surprisingly, there still are, although there's less ballet now and more jazz ballet and ballroom dancing.

Even in the past, Salvio's was one of the few shops around that made dance shoes, and as well as shoes for the local dance schools, it also supplied to shoe shops in country towns. But little shops in the middle of nowhere are finding it too hard to pay their bills now, and Salvio's can't afford to deal with them anymore. And along with the change in clientele, these days, those ballet flats are just as likely to be used for streetwear as they are in dance studios; to be seen in the pages of fashion magazines as on the feet of ballerinas. And a certain number of flamenco shoes – like the ones I bought – are made without nails in the soles ('Your neighbours will hate you if you have nails,' Ted's daughter Cathy Lennox tells me) and are never seen on stage.

When Ted Salvio plays golf on Mondays and Fridays he wears a pair of golfing shoes he made himself. A black patent-leather toe, white leather uppers and black round the heel. Spikes on the sole. 'The guys have a shot at me – they call them my dancing shoes – but I can wear it.' For the rest of the week he wears Salvio's aerobic shoes – in black or white.

Ted's wife, June, is wearing a pair of specially made black aerobic shoes with a gently wedged sole. Cathy Lennox, who took time out to be a medical secretary but has been working in the shop since her now adult daughters were babies, never wears anything but Salvio's, 'except sandshoes for netball and Crocs for gardening'. Her brother and sister don't work in the business, neither do her two daughters. 'You want something different for your own children, but you never know, one day we might have grandchildren who take it over.' She's got dozens of pairs of Salvio's shoes. If someone stops her in the street and asks where she bought them, 'I tell them they were from a ballet shop in Randwick, I don't say it's my shop.' Only Cathy's husband, Phil Lennox, who runs the factory, is wearing something different. A pair of trainers the size of refrigerators, with soles made of old tyres. 'They're the only things that'll keep the tacks out,' he says, turning his foot over to show what he means. They're so shot with metal he could use them for tap shoes. He's got a 'nice pair of brogues', he says, for when he goes out.

When we visit, he's working on boots for Jupiters Casino's next show. Thirty years ago, when he first started, 'all we did was pink ballet shoes, black ballet shoes, tap shoes, jazz shoes – that's all we ever did'. Now, he says, there's always something

BOOKS

4E

different, and he couldn't imagine doing anything else. Even if they won Lotto, say Phil Lennox and Ted Salvio, there's no way they'd stop working. 'No, we had a saying years ago, "You've got to think of the ballet girls." We couldn't do it to them.'

Not long ago, Salvio's made the tap shoes for *Billy Elliot*. Ted and June Salvio go and see the shows when they can. 'With *Billy Elliot*, we were sitting there wondering when they were going to use the tap shoes,' says Ted. 'It was in the finale, there they all were on stage, going for their lives.' He's very pleased, he says, to see his shoes in action, not that they've been able to see them all. There were the shoes for the Moscow Circus – 'We made acrobatic shoes for them' – and cancan boots for a French troupe. 'If you can send our cancan boots to France, there must be something right about them.' And shoes for a Malaysian dance company and Opera Australia. Or '350 pairs of shoes that looked like they weren't wearing shoes at all for the film *Rapanui* – we had seven days to do them'. There's a romance to that, how someone from the Moscow Circus would have ever stumbled upon Salvio's in the first place, given that people who live streets away are unaware of its existence. But it turns out it's more mundane than you want it to be. Most of it's done on the internet – agents search internationally for companies who can deliver the right quantities of high-quality shoes at the right price, and Salvio's is often the one. 'We're $100 cheaper than most of the overseas companies. Another of the attractions is that we can make dozens of pairs of shoes for them – it's no problem.'

One of the oddest collaborations for Salvio's was when a tag team of wrestlers – 'one six foot six, the other five foot' – came into the shop, where you can hear the sounds of hammering from upstairs, and ordered boots. Into the shop that's papered in the same beige wallpaper put up nearly 40 years ago to cover the nicotined walls, and lined with shelves of flimsy cardboard shoeboxes, with the label with a dancer's silhouette on the end that was designed longer ago than anyone can remember but is starting to look smartly retro now. 'The two of them had crocodile-type outfits and you can't describe the boots, they were almost like crocodiles, quite way-out but that was what they wanted,' says Ted Salvio.

He can't think of any type of shoe Salvio's couldn't make – he points out a pair of sandals being made for a woman with a foot shaped like a football; and there's nothing simpler than making ballet shoes for a bunioned foot. 'Just add a bit to the last – that's all you have to do.'

SALVIO
2

When you get yourself fitted for a pair of shoes at Salvio's, no measurements are taken. 'We used to have one of those wooden measuring sticks years ago – it wasn't a fancy one – but I wouldn't know how to use it,' says Cathy Lennox. Instead, you just try on various shoes, and say how they feel – too narrow here, too big there. From there, your order's taken and a pair of shoes is made for you within weeks.

Technology doesn't come into Salvio's; there's nothing fancy about the way they do anything. Shoes are made the same way they've always been made. It's only the customers who use technology. While we're there, a little girl comes into the shop with her father to pick up her first pair of ballet slippers. They take them out of the shop and the man takes out his mobile phone. The girl holds up her ballet shoes and he takes a photo, and sends it off somewhere, who knows where.

Stonemason

The light in Ruben Varfi's studio is soft for a Sydney summer. He holds his hand out over a massive block of sandstone to show us how gentle, almost European, the light is. You can make out the barest trace of a shadow. Not much has been done to the corrugated iron shed in the grounds of the Centenary Stonework Program complex at Alexandria in Sydney to turn it into a studio – a few sheets of corrugated iron roofing have been replaced with clear sheeting, waist-high benches installed around the walls.

On one wall hangs a collage of photos and drawings of pineapples and bunya nuts. The pineapples are shown on buildings and banisters, fabric and wallpaper; the bunya nuts do not hold such a place in design history. On the opposite wall are photocopied photographic portraits of a state politician at various stages in his career, from early middle age to old age; a plaster bust of the man – Ruben Varfi can't remember who he

is – sits on a bench. He's chosen to sculpt him as he veers towards old age, youthful flesh no longer on his bones but instantly recognisable as the man in the photos. He may never be more than the plaster bust, says sculptor Ruben Varfi – the block of stone for the finished sculpture was going to cost $10,000.

In the middle of the space, Ruben Varfi, who was educated at a selective art high school in Albania and went back to teach at one for 20 years after studying at an art academy, is working on a commission by the Sydney Cove Redevelopment Authority for the Rockpool building on George Street. The studio was set up for this piece, to give Ruben Varfi, who's been at the Centenary Stonework Program for 10 of the 12 years he has lived in Australia, the best conditions to work in. 'I need to concentrate – in the other place, too much noise. Radio – I don't like radio.' He's talking about the other, larger, workspace, in a shed nearby, where half a dozen stonemasons manipulate blocks of sandstone, using hand tools and power tools to transform them into architectural features – pilasters and balusters, windowsills and capitals.

Ruben Varfi is wearing goggles and a dust mask. There's a vacuum cleaner, not much bigger than the average domestic one, behind him, and a three-dimensional model of the work. With a power tool that sounds painfully like a dentist's drill (a set of bits he designed for a drill are, in fact, based on those used by dentists), and causes slivers of sandstone to fly and a firework of sparks, he's clearing away stone from the bunches of grapes drawn lightly onto the surface of the four-metre-long block. A stylised pineapple is also drawn onto it – it won out over the bunya nut – as well as garlanded curlicues. Regular sections are marked off and numbered in chalk down the side of the stone. 'I start from one end and work to the other,' says Ruben Varfi.

It's an impressive piece of stone, as finely grained as salt and uniform in colour, slightly warm, with none of the brash yellow found in inferior versions of Sydney's bedrock. Ruben Varfi will go in later with hand tools to do the more precise work.

The Centenary Stonework Program was set up by the State Government in 1991 to cope with the backlog of maintenance work needed on various state-owned sandstone structures. Sydney, if you look at most of the old buildings and structures in the CBD and nearby suburbs, is a sandstone city. The Art Gallery of New South Wales, Central Railway Station, the State Library, Government House, Bourke Street Public School, various statues and war memorials around the place. It's a mellow material and

much softer than granite and marble and other stones used for buildings in Europe. It's so soft it's unlikely there'd be much for archaeologists to work with if they came across Sydney in a few thousand years.

The 'centenary' part of the name comes from Government Architect Walter Liberty Vernon, who forecast in 1899 that the city's sandstone buildings would need maintenance 'in about 100 years'. He was right. Once you're aware of the Centenary Stonework Program, you start noticing its scaffolding and banners everywhere. It's not just in the restoration of buildings and monuments but in walls and statues, stairways and kerbs. Weather, sea spray, pollution and human use predictably wear away the stone, but damage also happens in more precarious spots, such as the plinths to fencing around Centennial Park from cars veering off the roadway.

When stonemasons are working on buildings, they'll often find messages from previous workers. One stonemason talks about unearthing a 1972 business card in a plastic tub on a job in the city. 'We'll often leave a key or a coin in a join and grout it up for someone to find later – it's a good tradition.'

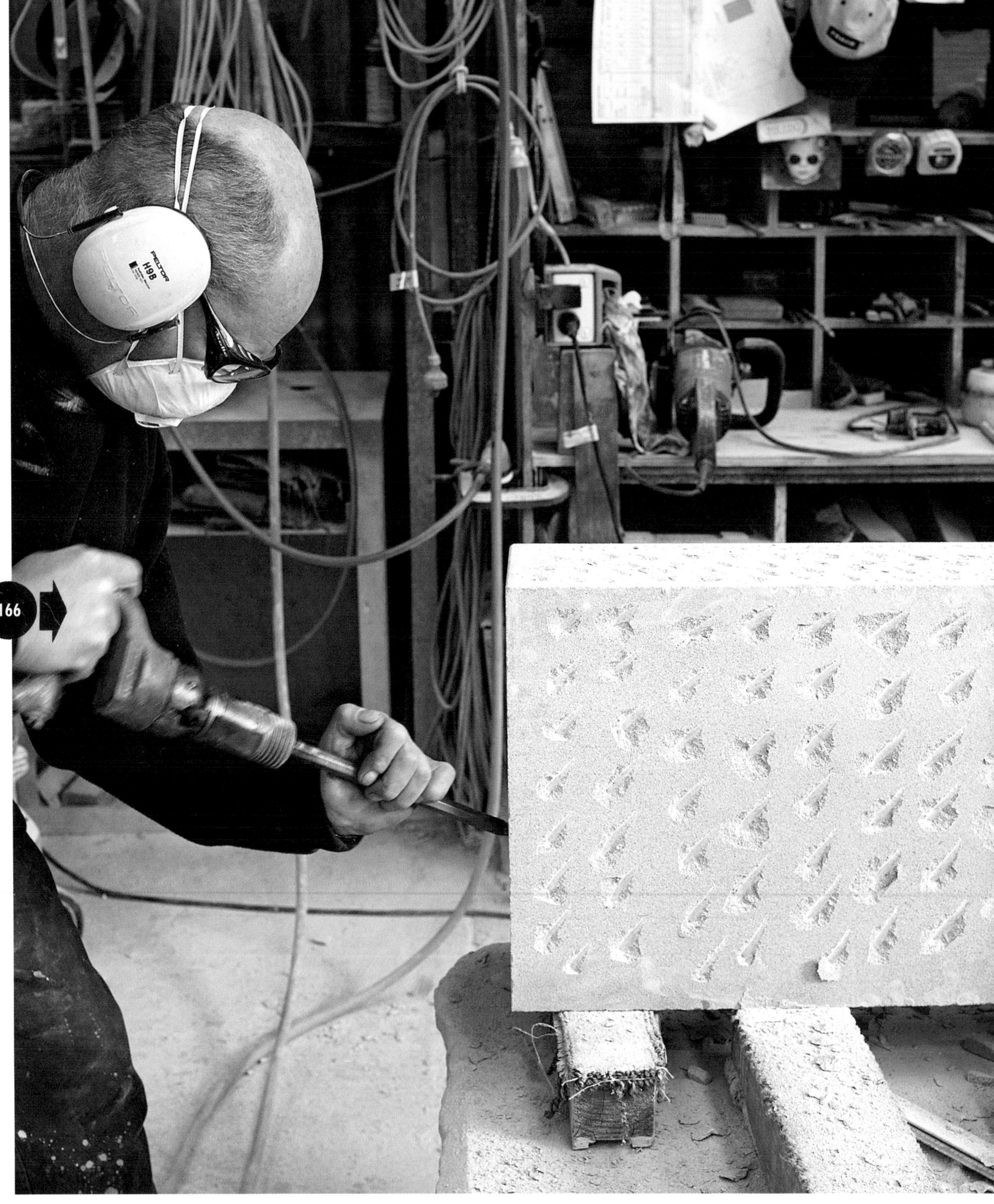
PELTOR
H9B

When Vernon was Government Architect, stonemasonry was a steady trade in Sydney. By the time his prediction was starting to be realised in the second half of last century, there were hardly any stonemasons left – the trade, like the sandstone buildings, was clearly out of fashion. Stonemasonry had been, says architect Ron Powell, manager of the program, 'the prima donna of the trades – is it an art or a craft? It was the first trade to negotiate 10- and eight-hour days, but also a trade in which in the 1800s, the average lifespan for workers was 45, because of diseases like silicosis.'

As well as stonemasons literally dying out, sandstone buildings and arcades were being flattened to make way for modern concrete towers; one of Sydney's more flamboyant sandstone structures, the Queen Victoria Building, was almost torn down several times, most shockingly in the late Fifties for a city square and underground parking. Mayor at the time Harry Jensen's justification was that 'the Queen Victoria Building site is magnificent – and the building makes inadequate use of it'. An editorial in the *Sydney Morning Herald* agreed with him on social and aesthetic grounds, and urged the council to support the Lord Mayor, but the idea was, thankfully, postponed and eventually shelved.

In an outdoor area at the stoneyard, geologists' core boxes, about the size of suitcases and made of tin, are divided into slender compartments containing cylinders of three-hundred-million-year-old sandstone ('made when this was still Gondwanaland', says Ron Powell), each one marked to show which sites in the city they were taken from. I'm drawn to the cylinders I can see time in – the ones with rippling layers of varying colours and textures, with streaks of quartz clearly visible. I'm sure I can see leaves in there, too. They're the poorest quality, says Ron Powell. 'The best comes from sites with six to seven metres of undifferentiated stone, formed by the mother of all floods over a matter of weeks, with some of the material coming from 700 kilometres away.' Those cylinders look manmade they're so perfect.

For the Centenary Stonework Program to look after the more than 600 buildings and monuments made partly, or completely, from sandstone (some are of brick with a sandstone trim), it needs supplies of sandstone. At the yard, a warehouse is set aside for part of the stockpile of blocks, some the size of buses, collected from Sydney's old quarries and building sites. Buzz-saws, as tall as people, slice the blocks into manageable sizes. Paradise, Purgatory and Hell Hole the three main quarries were called, and they were all in Pyrmont and developed in the middle of the nineteenth century. Most, but not all, of Sydney's greatest public buildings came from Paradise sandstone, which is probably the best in the world. Government House, in the Botanic Gardens, was built in the 1830s, before Paradise's time. 'The stone comes from the site, and from Goat Island,' says Ron Powell. 'It's not great stone.'

Paradise was under the old CSR site which, like many parts of the inner-city, has now been turned over to apartments. Before that new complex was built, the Centenary Stonework Program made a deal with the developers and excavated, carefully extracting the valuable stone in enormous, usable pieces rather than letting it be shattered into useless landfill-sized chunks. There are 6000 blocks, or about 20 years' worth, of sandstone at the yard, but the program is always looking for more. What happened at Paradise should happen at every major building site around Sydney – the Sydney City Council has recently made it a requirement that developers excavate carefully.

The Centenary Stonework Program is also set up to train stonemasons, to carry on the work of George Proudman, a stonemason who started an apprenticeship scheme in the Seventies. From just a handful of tradesmen, all on the verge of retirement, the program is cultivating whole new generations of stonemasons, with several new apprentices each year, who learn on the job, guided by some of the experts at the Alexandria yard. Guided by people like Ruben Varfi and master mason Afonso Pires, who comes from Portugal and started his working life making hundreds of kerbstones by hand for the Algarve town of Bordeira. When he arrived in Australia in 1968, Afonso Pires was on the Leyland production line for a year before finding work as a stonemason in Sydney.

The newer apprentices are smoothing out the saw lines from blocks of stone with carborundum and water, one of the first jobs they ever have to do and one in which they start to have a feel for the material they work with. In other parts of the large shed, open at both ends to the light and big enough that you'd need to shout to be heard between benches, are partly finished pilasters and other architectural details and – a weekend project – an entry by one of the stonemasons into Sculpture by the Sea. It looks like an exhibit at a natural history museum, with fossilised skeletons emerging from a raw lump of rock.

'I love carving, it keeps me sane,' says Paul Thurlowe, who has been production manager of the program for nine years. It keeps a lot of people sane, he says. He's not the only one who comes in after-hours to work on projects. Even Ron Powell, when we visit the yard, is about to go off on holiday to look at stone churches and cathedrals around England.

Katie Hicks is working on corbels for Sydney Hospital. She's using a mallet and chisel, but tools and jobs have different names in stonemasonry. Pitcher, scutch, banker mason (a mason who works in the studio), fixer mason (one who works directly on the buildings). Tools and names that have been around for centuries. Air guns and angle grinders have been added to the mix.

Katie Hicks was studying criminology when she read Ken Follett's *The Pillars of the Earth*, a novel set in mediaeval times about the building of a cathedral, and became obsessed with the idea of becoming a stonemason. She rang every stonemason in the phone book before being taken on at the Centenary Stonework Program. That was in 1999, and since then her work has included the date stone for Paddington Public School, a cross for a Ryde church and the top of a column in Centennial Park. 'I sometimes show friends what I've done – it's a good feeling to know it's going to be there for a long time.' When she goes home, covered in the white sandstone dust, Katie Hicks dyes textiles, makes felt, and knits. 'I like to be surrounded by vibrant colour, and the softness of those things – it's a contrast.'

Elfin Cars

Elfin is not like most factories. Most factories keep the doors closed and don't encourage visitors to wander in. The first time I went to the Elfin factory a few years ago to do an article for a newspaper magazine, a retired businessman was there watching his MS8 Streamliner being built by hand. He had an album of photos documenting the whole process – a snap of the contract being signed, another of the chassis being laid down, and on it went. He'd just decided on its colour – red – he'd be back a few weeks later to take a shot of his car being painted.

He'd owned three Elfins before this one – his first in 1963 when he was a racing driver. He visited the Elfin factory on the edge of Melbourne's Moorabbin Airport every week or two to check on his car's progress. He wasn't unusual; many men, and it is pretty well always men, who order Elfins, drop in regularly to watch their cars being built, often flying from the other side of the country to do so.

The name Elfin doesn't mean a thing to most Australians. But to anyone interested in motor sport, it's a different matter. It's a brand of hand-built Australian racing car, first cobbled together in the late Fifties by Garrie Cooper in his Adelaide workshop. Named after the engines of the model aeroplanes he used to fly, Elfins fulfilled their definition of being 'small spritely creatures possessing magical powers'.

The cars were light, fast – Australia's answer to the Lotus Seven – and, above all, affordable, making it possible for enthusiasts without pots of money to run competitively against men who could afford imported cars. Garrie Cooper was regarded as a god.

For a while in the Sixties, Elfin was the second-largest manufacturer of racing cars in the world – Formula One champion James Hunt drove one, so, too did some of the big names of Australian racing. Until Cooper's death in 1982, almost 250 cars, of various designs, had rolled out of his workshop, winning many races along the way.

After languishing for a number of years, the company was bought by Melbourne motoring man Murray Richards, who had almost finished building the prototype of a road-registrable Elfin Clubman before he had to stop working because of ill health. A clothing manufacturer wanted to buy the marque, but Richards decided to sell it to a couple of car nuts, Bill Hemming, an ex-ad man, and Nick Kovatch, a weekend racer.

To start with, the pair developed the Clubman Type 3, an open-wheeled sports car based on Cooper and Richards' designs. (The Clubman is a lightweight, minimalist car, made by a number of individuals around the world, and is basically an engine, gearbox and wheels which goes like the clappers.) They were making these at the rate of about 15 or 20 a year, in kit form for those who wanted to build it themselves, or hand-built in the factory.

They were also aiming higher – towards a more sophisticated range of cars. And that happened quite by chance in 2001 when a prospective customer came into the factory to look at a Clubman. He took one for a drive, said he liked it but reckoned he could design something better.

Two weeks later, when he came back with a few sketches, Bill Hemming and Nick Kovatch realised he knew what he was talking about. That's when Mike Simcoe, at the time design director of Holden Design in Melbourne, introduced himself. The sketches were for a new generation Clubman, still open-wheeled and minimalist but

ITEM:
QTY:
NW:
GW:
MEA'T
US-175
HT

merging the traditional and brand new, and much better than anything Hemming and Kovatch could have imagined.

And so it was the start of a very odd relationship – a huge multinational helping out a tiny company. Mike Simcoe used Holden resources and got his design team working on the new car. Initially it was done on the side before Holden became involved legitimately, seeing it as an opportunity to present itself as a company with a heart. It was a way of keeping passion and motivation in the design team, and also gave Elfin the expertise to help them through the impenetrable Australian Design Rules, essential when you're trying to build a road-registrable car.

Mike Simcoe's team went on to design the MS8 Streamliner (with optional soft- or hard-top), launched alongside the Clubman at the 2004 Melbourne motor show and a much more aggressive and modern-looking vehicle. The two cars were a big hit at the show, and continued to generate enormous interest internationally.

So much so that eventually Bill Hemming and Nick Kovatch were bought out in 2006 by Walkinshaw Performance, led by Scotsman Tom Walkinshaw, best known for his involvement on the international motor racing circuit.

When I rang Gary Beer, sales and marketing executive of the company, I was concerned. 'We've made it far more of a production-line operation,' he said, and talked of 'production efficiencies'. I could only imagine what that meant.

When I'd been down to Elfin in 2005, the handmade nature of the cars was evident. Virtually every bit of the car, from the aluminium and fibreglass panels, painted in the specially mixed colour of the client's choice, down to the leather seats (modified to suit customers' weights and heights), was custom-built in the small workshop.

I needn't have worried. Not much had changed since I'd last been there. The only differences I can see are that the racing car restoration business Nick Kovatch ran in one corner of the factory isn't there anymore, and the kits are no longer made.

Gary Beer is mad about cars, as everyone who works at Elfin is. 'You need to be,' he says. 'When a customer comes in, he should be able to talk to anyone about his car, and have a better experience than if he was buying from a caryard.'

The factory is looking as uncluttered as it ever was – there's no yard out the back with stock waiting to go to dealers – each car is still built to order, and leaves as soon as it is finished. Only four or five cars, at the most, are being built at one time, and individual taste can be seen in the metallic turquoise Clubman with yellow stripe, partly assembled, and the lurid orange body of another car in one corner of the works. Elfin cars may be pared back to the bare bones in some respects – air conditioning and heating optional, no extraneous padding, an elegantly minimal dashboard – but there's nothing understated about certain choices.

Since Walkinshaw took over the operation of Elfin, some of the more extreme aspects of the cars have been toned down: 'They were very focused for the track,' says Gary Beer. 'We've taken out the really high end racing componentry and replaced it with something more roadworthy.' But still, he says, many people do liken driving an Elfin to 'riding a motorcycle with the safety and comfort of four wheels'.

You can never forget what you're dealing with at the Elfin factory, says Gary Beer. 'We're not making widgets or buckets, we're making something that's extremely quick, extremely dangerous.' And it's for that reason the place is as tidy and spotless as it is. There isn't a tool, a piece of equipment or a component out of place, and, says Gary Beer, you could eat your lunch off the floor. 'We're dealing with people's lives here – you need to have faith in our product.'

The production line Gary Beer talked about on the phone is, thankfully, just a series of four tables in the middle of the factory floor. There's plenty of space around them. In an area beyond the tables, men are welding together a chassis from components that look like a large-scale Meccano kit. A strange skeleton is emerging.

At each of the tables in the production line, a man is working on a car at a certain stage of its creation. It's like an operating theatre, as each man goes about his job seriously and methodically. It's as quiet as a bookbinder's in here. There's no screeching or thumping of power tools the day I visit the Elfin factory, no need to wear ear muffs. The only tools being used are spanners and screwdrivers, operated entirely by hand. For a car factory, this doesn't seem too far removed from an Adelaide workshop in the Fifties.

THIN

Tannery

If you've driven through the Arch of Victory on the road out of Ballarat, you've gone too far for Greenhalgh Tannery. As the town thins out, the arch is there, strangely grandiose and over-scaled. Built in 1920, it spans the whole road and marks the beginning of the tree-lined Avenue of Honour, commemorating the 3771 soldiers from the area who served in the First World War.

The road to Greenhalgh Tannery – from a turn-off just before the arch – is long and straight and flat. A few cows in fields, a few new houses with names like Kensington, not much else. The road is called Greenhalghs Road. 'All we need now is a town called Greenhalgh and we're right,' says Bruce Greenhalgh, who runs the tannery with his brother, Ross. He's not pushing for it. 'I don't think anyone would be terribly interested.'

The tannery is out on its own, away from the houses. A sign on the gate says it's open from seven-thirty to noon and from one to six. A week after the 2009 Black Saturday Victorian bushfires, it's windy and drizzling and unseasonably cold on Greenhalghs Road.

Greenhalgh Tannery, about 10 kilometres from the centre of Ballarat, is made up of series of corrugated iron sheds, some open to one side, all different sizes, dumped in a paddock, muddy pathways between. It looks like a haphazard nineteenth century settlement. It's not – some of the sheds are only a few years old. There's a shop at the tannery selling ugg boots and belts, sheepskin rugs and bullock-hide rugs, tanned hides. The tanned hides and rugs are made at the tannery; the rest are brought in.

This is a business that has been in the family for generations. Bruce Greenhalgh's great-great-grandfather came out from Britain and operated a tannery outside Smythesdale, near Ballarat. 'He moved into Ballarat and his son eventually came here,' says Bruce Greenhalgh, a big bloke who looks at home in a tannery. It was around the time of the Ballarat gold rush, when there were tanneries all over the countryside, that Greenhalgh set up, making leather primarily for bridles and saddles. And that's the leather it continues to make today. Whether the tannery stays as a family business remains to be seen. Ross Greenhalgh has two children, too young yet to show much interest in the company, and Bruce is 'a bachelor – I'm a crop failure, if you like'. And if the houses get much closer, the residents may object to having a smelly and hardly picturesque plant nearby, even if it has been there for years.

Bruce Greenhalgh used to come over to the tannery as a young boy 'and wanted to do what Dad did, I suppose. I wasn't that keen on further education, so I suppose I came here.' It's a life, he says, that 'does have a bit of variety to it. You get different people coming. Sometimes what they want and what they're doing with the product surprises me – the different straps, the rocking horse saddles and all sorts of things. The whips.'

Not much has changed about the tannery operation since it started more than a century and a half ago. It's one of the few places left in Australia still tanning with wattle bark, which comes in looking like massive tea leaves.

Skins, in selected weights, are brought up to the tannery from a hide store in Melbourne. On wooden pallets, the anaemic objects sit like stacks of folded blankets. They're heavy hides – suitable for harnesses and bridles; too solid for a pair of shoes. They've already been brined and salted, says Bruce Greenhalgh. I can imagine what he means. And they've been pre-fleshed, too. 'Before, we had to flesh them ourselves.' He has to explain. 'We'd put them through a thing called a fleshing machine, which

takes the fat and bits of meat off. But now we're not buying a whole heap of fat and rubbish.' The fleshing machine, still there in one of the sheds, is caked and dripping with congealed fat; the smell is rancidly sweet. The animal that is the hide becomes appallingly apparent.

It's a gruesome business, tanning. The pre-fleshed hides are put in lime pits for three or four days 'to plump them up and loosen the hair'. Ropes are attached to the corners of the hides, so they can be agitated in the pits, 'and to drag them back in again'. From there, they go into a scudding machine, like a front-loader washing machine, which takes the hair off, and are bathed in an ammonia solution to bring them back to their natural thickness. 'My grandfather saved the hair and used it for stuffing things, or would sell it to put in plaster for plastering walls. Dad used it for carpet underlay once. We could use it now but it's not worth it – too much work to collect it.'

It's once they've been in the ammonia solution that the hides are sunk into the pits of wattle bark for weeks. 'Years ago it would have taken longer,' says Bruce Greenhalgh. 'In Britain they'd use acorns or oak bark and it would take about 12 months.' The wattle bark is mixed with water in liquor pits to make a brackish tea. 'It doesn't dissolve, the colour is from the tannin coming out.' Racks of hides, looking like the trays in oyster leases, are left in there for six to eight weeks, first in a weak solution of wattle bark tea and gradually building up to the strongest. A pump keeps the tea on the move, and the hides draw in the tannin to produce the tough leather required for saddlery, and for embossing. Tanned with wattle bark, says Bruce Greenhalgh, 'the leather doesn't stretch as much as it does with other compounds, and it can be moulded'. The used wattle bark, he says, can be thrown on the garden for mulch.

Up around the pits, a flurry of leather offcuts, the size of oak leaves, litters the ground. Every week, about 40 hides are tanned at Greenhalgh. Nearly all are cattle, but occasionally they do other skins as special orders: goat, deer, kangaroo. They once did a lion skin for a museum. 'It wasn't difficult,' says Bruce Greenhalgh. 'It was much the same as any other hairy hide.' Alpacas and merino sheep, animals with very fine hair, are the tricky ones, he says. 'You agitate the hides and the hair matts down – it needs to be combed out, and that's hard.'

The tanned hides are rinsed in a drum, wrung out in a wringer, split in a machine to make them of an even thickness, and dyed in a water-tank-sized wooden barrel.

In a drying shed, dyed hides are tacked to vertical racks made of timber and chicken wire. In some weathers they're steam-dried; at other times of year they dry naturally. A bucket of rusty nails is by the doorway. A few steps away are some fresh cow pats. So, animals do wander around here. 'Yes, they're doomed, aren't they,' says Bruce Greenhalgh.

The finished hides, stacked on shelves by weight and colour in another shed, look like cardboard. One shelf holds hides dyed the colour of cricket balls. They're beautiful. 'You wouldn't think so if you worked with them,' says Bruce Greenhalgh. 'The red comes off on your hands.' On a long bench, petroleum jelly is rubbed into the hides to soften them. 'Otherwise they'd be like pieces of tin.' An embossing press in the shed is used to imprint the pore pattern seen on bags and wallets. Hides, says Bruce Greenhalgh, are naturally smooth. 'They've got their own character to them, sometimes you'll find brands in there.' He draws his hand over a seemingly perfect hide lying on the bench and points to growth marks around the rump and, along a flank, a pale trace of the creature's encounter with a faraway barbed wire fence.

Art Supplies

Thirty years ago David Keys was regularly flying between Australia and New Zealand on business. At 30,000 feet above the Tasman, he couldn't help noticing the colour of the ocean and sky – it seemed very particular to that part of the world. You could cross the English Channel a million times and never see that shade, he says. David Keys has a business making, among many art supplies, oil paints for artists. On those trips he decided to try to replicate that blue in a paint colour. He'd mix up what he thought was right in his Melbourne workshop, take it on board next time he was flying, find out he was wrong and try again the following time. It took about six flights before he'd got anywhere near it – 'colour's very elusive, like musical notes' – before he'd created that 'smoky, very faint blue with incredible depth. There's a lot of shallow water in the Tasman, so you get a lot of bounce back of light, which affects the atmosphere. I forget how I did it now, it was an accident – I put something in it that I'd never dream of, and it gave that mystery effect.'

The name of the paint – Tasman Blue. The names of Art Spectrum's colours are like that – along with Italian Pink and Terre Verte are names such as Pilbara Red and Flinders Blue Violet. Before Art Spectrum started making paints, all oil paints for artists came from overseas. 'We live in such a colourful continent, in which the red earth at Uluru was red millions of years ago and it's still red, that it seemed odd that no one was making artists' colours,' says David Keys, who's sitting in his office in a drab low-slung brick building, housing the administrative and warehouse side of the business, opposite a park on a quiet Melbourne street. Vertical louvres are at the windows; small jars of powdered pigment, the colours of butterflies' wings, line the shelves of a cabinet; a bookcase is haphazardly filled with tubes of oil paints on stands. Tasman Blue is missing.

The story of Art Spectrum started before those trips across the Tasman, but information is as elusive as colour when talking to artist David Keys, who slides over details as mundane as dates, is sidetracked by talk of sonnets and cooking. He dates the story back to 'one Friday night' in Melbourne, but it begins about a year before that, in 1963, when he went to London on a British Council grant. At the time he was lecturing at the Royal Melbourne Institute of Technology (RMIT) and had a painting in the National Gallery of Victoria, 'an abstract, I forget the title'. He left behind his wife and two children – 'she didn't want to go, and it's amazing how quickly the time went' – to become a visiting artist at the Slade. He taught there, and at St Martin's, at a time when his students were paying their fees by running drugs or 'painting nudes on wide ties', worked with an architect for a few months, visited Henry Moore and a few other artists and did some travelling, looking at art. 'I didn't want to waste any time, I was very conscious of the fact that I'd left my family behind. I didn't want to bugger it up.' His wife, Gay, and son David, who trained in town planning, now work with him.

He might have thought he'd made the most of his year away, but others saw it differently. 'When you go away from RMIT for 12 months, they regard it as a holiday, so give you all the crappy jobs when you come back.' At a life-drawing class on a Friday night with fashion students, who weren't particularly interested in life-drawing classes, he started thinking about alternatives.

Chats in the tea room with colleagues, who'd also spent time overseas, about the exorbitant cost, and poor supply, of paints and canvases in Melbourne set David Keys on the path to creating the forerunner of Art Spectrum. In those days, canvas had to be ordered from England, and would take at least six weeks to arrive and cost a week's salary. Artists, except for the well-off ones, he says, were painting on anything they could get their hands on; masonite or cardboard 'with a bit of house paint, and refrigerator boxes, because they were so big, were popular'. David Keys and his colleagues talked about doing something about it. 'I'm a doer, I don't like just talking about things. I take after my father, who came out from England, went broke twice during the Depression and then set up an engineering works. I'm a tenacious bastard.'

He collected £100 from half a dozen colleagues, went off to the almost derelict Davies Coop factory, which had been making tents and firehoses, organised to get some old machinery up and running again, and had some canvas woven. 'I've still got some of it today – it's priceless, beautiful stuff, heavy yarn, tightly woven, equal warp and weft. That taught me an awful lot about weaving canvas.'

The original plan was to just make enough canvas for themselves 'at a laughable price'. But they started cutting it up and selling it to students. 'We nearly got into trouble because we weren't a registered company and weren't paying tax; initiative can be a dangerous thing.' Before long, they needed to get another lot woven, 'and then we realised we had nothing to stretch it on, so we had to make some stretchers'.

David Keys bought 'a huge pile of timber', a machine for cutting it, which he still has, and spent his daytimes teaching and painting, night-times making the stretchers, getting some instruction from a framer at the National Gallery. 'We learnt all about it as we went – we didn't know what sort of wood to use, how the wood should be dried, what sort of corners to do and so on.'

Business was building up as schools and other institutions were ordering, so much so that a company was officially set up. 'We called it Stretchers Ltd, but people thought they were for carrying bodies on, so we called it Art Stretchers.'

The next step was to design a gesso-type surface to go on the canvas, and then to find somewhere to store it all, eventually opening a shop on Queensberry Place. 'It was a funny old place, an Aladdin's cave, everybody loved it – they still talk nostalgically about it.' The shop was also selling artists' paints from England – 'that's all there was then' – until 'Dear old Blackie', a Professor Black from Melbourne University, suggested they make their own. 'Being a professor of chemistry, it was a pushover for him,' he says, and mentions something about getting bones from the butcher and

burning them. David Keys had made paint very badly when he was a student, using pigment and buying the wrong type of linseed oil at the hardware shop – 'the stuff you'd put on cricket bats' – but gradually read up on the subject, and got some tips from the professor. In those days, he used a triple mill – a machine with three rollers, each rotating in the opposite direction to the next – only about 40 centimetres wide to thoroughly mill and coat pigment particles in the oil, 'but it almost shook the first floor out of the brick wall at Queensberry Place'.

Now, in a factory close to the office, a much larger triple mill, and paint mixers – like kitchen mixers but hundreds of times the size – show remnants of paint made over the years. Pastels in chalky colours are squeezed out of a machine and lined up on sheets of kitchen paper like expensive sweets.

At Queensberry Place, the paint tubes were filled by hand – 'I look back and it seems silly' – now, it's all done by machine. And, in a glass-fronted laboratory, a forensic chemist 'who works with the police does all the company's chemistry', making sure the paints and other products do what they're meant to do.

It wasn't David Keys' intention to make Australian colours – the original plan was purely to make paint locally so there wasn't the lag in deliveries from the other side of the world. But gradually southern hemisphere shades crept in, as he saw a need. 'I made an Australian grey – the grey on a gum tree, which isn't grey at all, it's a warm off-white. I made a good transparent black that doesn't make colours dirty.' In England you have to make colours dirty. 'They're lovely, but subdued, colours.' Occasionally, on a rare English summer's day, the colours will brighten – and it's then local artists could do with a tube of Tasman Blue or Pilbara Red, made with pigments from a Bavarian company. Art Spectrum sends its products everywhere, including England – when we visit, shipments are leaving the warehouse for New Jersey and Fiji, Bateman's Bay, NSW, and Murarrie, Queensland.

For a while, says David Keys, it was hard to stop making colours. When you've done it successfully once or twice, you want to keep going. 'I had to pull myself up, I started to do things that weren't useful.' They were colours that could be mixed on a palette by 'putting a bit of this and a bit of that'. Manufacturing a separate colour in such a case, he says, 'messes up the philosophy of keeping it as simple as possible'. He likens making paints to cooking. 'I like cooking, but don't like cooking from a cookery

book. I like getting something nice and fresh from my own garden and thinking what I'll do with it. It's the same thing – good materials, you put them together and something comes out of it.'

As the number of paints in Art Spectrum's catalogue grew, so have other product lines – canvases woven in Belgium, watercolours, paper milled by a family company in Italy, pastels 'extra soft like paint, and designed to be something Degas would like to have used', brushes, made all over the world, some designed by David Keys, pencils. 'We try to invent new things that artists use and need, nothing gimmicky.'

For years David Keys has tried to keep up with his own painting, but he now has, he says, hundreds of unfinished canvases waiting for attention. Business has been an intrusion at times, 'but then I realised that doing this firm is another sort of creativity. I've had to talk myself into it sometimes that this is another kind of canvas, which is exactly what it is.'

Now in his eighties, he's at the office every day, he's 'interested in life' and always looking for the next challenge. He recently picked up a 'thick Penguin book on the history of sonnets' at a bookshop near the factory, took it home, read a few and decided to write one in the next few months. 'There's a format and discipline to it, you can't wander off and do anything you like.'

He's well aware that the company that started by accident could just as easily disappear after he's gone. 'That's life, bugger it. Life matters while you're here, you do your best, but people stuck on dynasties – you only have to read histories of ancient Greece, or England, France, Germany, to see the ups and downs are what makes it interesting.'

Foundry

The walls of the office at Central Foundry are covered with closely spaced panels of wrought-iron lacework. It's like wallpaper. Intricate patterns of leaves, stylised urns, diamond borders, Australian native flowers. They're samples of work available at the foundry, and the only thing that passes for decoration here.

Central Foundry is a family company, set up in 1940 not far from where it is now, near Sydney Airport. The building it's been in since the early Nineties used to be a tyre factory. Mark Boyle and his twin brothers, Justin and John, work there. So does his father, Kevin. And his mother, Jan, works in the office. His uncle and his two cousins worked there until five or six years ago. 'They were going in a different direction,' says Mark Boyle. 'My uncle had had enough by that stage.'

It's easy to understand why anyone would be less than enthusiastic about being in a foundry – it's as hot and grimy as any workplace could possibly be, a vision of hard labour. Faces and limbs are shadowed in black dust – remnants of black sand used in the casting process; a vat holding molten aluminium (from ingots, stacked up and cartoonish in their brilliance) glows a fluorescent orange; men are shovelling a heavy load of sand into a mould, compacting it around a pattern for a drawer handle.

Once an imprint of the pattern is made, it's removed, and the sand, which is mixed with a hardener, dries. Tracks, designed differently for each mould, are cut through it for the molten metal to flow. There's an art to pouring molten metal and predicting how it will solidify – the pouring has to be controlled and contained, allowing the metal to flow smoothly so it doesn't create dross as it cools down. Pour too quickly or too slowly and you can end up with slag, which happens when it picks up oxides and nitrogen. The same thing can happen if the molten metal is overheated. 'There's a thousand things that can go wrong with the process, it's very complicated,' says Mark Boyle.

It seems impossibly complicated as Mark Boyle talks about it – he shows us various moulds lined up, and we watch as molten metal is ladled into them. The engineering and science of foundry work collides with the purely physical.

A mould created from sand can only be used once, as it breaks down in the high temperatures. (Die-casting with steel dies, an expensive process, is used when several thousand pieces are being made.)

For some jobs, black sand is used – and reused, recycled over and over again in the foundry. It travels on an underground conveyor belt to a mixer, where it's crushed and mixed with oil and clay. Normal beach sand is more difficult to recycle, says Mark Boyle, and is sent off and treated before going into landfill.

Technology has made its way into the foundry – induction furnaces use an electromagnetic field to melt some metals relatively cleanly – but the overwhelming impression is of an industry that has scarcely changed in 100 years. Someone, almost romantically, mentioned *Battleship Potemkin* at the thought of a traditional foundry (they hadn't got the right film but I recognised the sentiment); it was a stifling place to be on a December day, and the smell of chemical change lingered in my clothes

202

for days. Mark Boyle says he has never heard of a woman doing heavy work in a foundry, although during the Second World War, he says, with the shortage of men in the local workforce, women were doing the less strenuous foundry jobs.

The Boyle family have been involved in foundries for almost a century, setting up their first business in 1913. Brothers Herb and Albert Boyle had already been running a foundry before that, but no one knows for quite how long that had been going. They had a rough time during the Depression – Albert had to work at another foundry for a few years – but managed to restart their business towards the end of the Thirties, and gradually acquired other foundries around Sydney.

There used to be around 20 foundries in the area where Central Foundry stands. Now, there's only one other left, another non-ferrous foundry, on the same road. 'We don't cross wires with them. He borrows stuff from us,' says Mark Boyle, who worked in foundries in Sheffield for a few years on a working holiday. There's another non-ferrous one a few kilometres away in Kirrawee, he says. 'We have a good relationship with him too. We'll ring each other for a chat, and we do work for each other.' All over New South Wales, he reckons, there would be around 20 foundries left altogether. The foundry business is, he says, a dying trade, 'and has been for a long time. A lot of people out there are looking for easier ways to make a dollar.'

A non-ferrous foundry, as the name suggests, deals with every metal but iron and steel. Temperature's got a lot to do with the difference between ferrous and non-ferrous foundries, says Mark Boyle. 'Steel is cast at about 1600 degrees, whereas the hottest we go is 1200 or 1250.' Ferrous foundries, he says, are often 'giant steel places that make 15,000 of this, 20,000 of that. Car parts and things. There are not many around that make one-offs, which is what we're still doing.' And which won't be made anymore, he believes, if all business goes offshore, which is already starting to happen.

On the small side, it's one-offs of the lacework, now made in aluminium, and one-off copies of antique drawer handles which people bring in. Then there's 'lots of mining equipment, engineering components and marine parts, fittings for boats in aluminium, bronze and brass.'

Its main business is with urban furniture – park benches and lamp poles and bus seats and railing – die-cast, as they're made by the hundred. The company has made bronze lights for the Sydney Opera House, and in-ground plaques around Circular

Quay detailing the lives of writers from Banjo Paterson to Peter Carey. Some of its clients include local councils and the defence department. Central Foundry has done work, too, for clients overseas – lacework on a resort for developers in Malaysia, machinery parts for a German company. Its materials, wherever possible, are Australian – aluminium from Tasmania, copper-based metals from the mainland.

And Central Foundry also makes yacht keels – big ones – and that has become one of the company's specialties. They're the largest things the foundry makes – the heaviest weighing up to 16 tonnes. 'You wouldn't think a boat would float with a thing like that. It was for *Leopard*, which came second in the Sydney to Hobart last year.' In the 10 years to 2009, the Sydney to Hobart Yacht Race has been won nine times by yachts with Central Foundry keels.

One of its most famous yachting collaborations was with Ben Lexcen. The foundry worked on scaled-down casting trials of the famous winged keel, and managed to keep it secret until *Australia II* had won the final four races of the America's Cup in 1983.

The foundry also works with artists on one-off sculptures, 'lots of strange jobs for Sculpture by the Sea, giant forks and other bizarre shapes – jobs like those are definitely the most interesting'. It also made the Giant Buddha for the temple in Wollongong – a massive piece, well over the height of the factory roof. 'We did it in sections and welded it together.' And so from the dark and heat and discomfort of Central Foundry, emerged a manganese bronze form weighing 4000 kilograms – gleaming and corpulent, and a powerful symbol of a belief system from a very different time and place.

Foundry

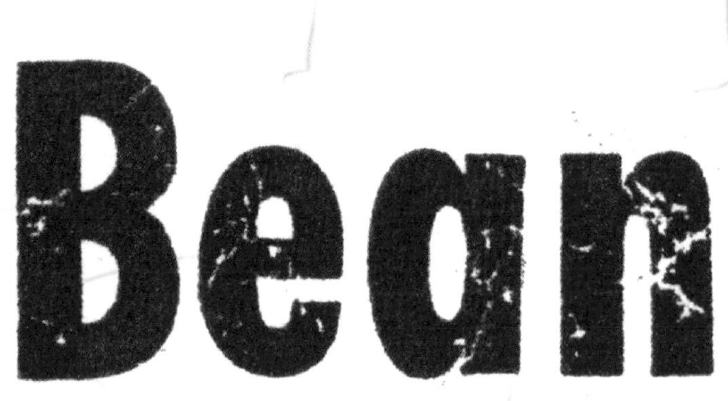

Bean Slicers

The population of the Réunion Islands is somewhere over 600,000. In its time, Tatham Cutlery has sold more than 600,000 Krisk Bean Slicers to the Réunion Islands. You can't help wondering what they do with them there.

'I don't know and I don't really care,' says director and production manager Mark Rowell quickly, and laughs. You can see his point.

Zimbabwe used to be another big market for the Krisk Bean Slicer, the home kitchen gadget that's been made in Australia since 1923. It turns out they used them to slice the beans that ended up in bags in English supermarket freezers. It appears whole factories can be set up with several dozen Krisk Bean Slicers, possibly a few chairs, and a steady supply of plastic bags.

South America's a big market for the Krisk Bean Slicer, so too are Portugal, Spain, England, Madagascar – 'anywhere they eat beans'. On the wall in the Tatham Cutlery office in Rydalmere, near Parramatta in Sydney's western suburbs, is a world map, the type you'd find in a classroom, stuck with pins of various colours showing where around the globe the Krisk Bean Slicer ends up. Of the 350,000 sold a year, not all that many, relatively speaking, stay in Australia these days. With a product almost as old as Vegemite, that's a shame. A lot of that has to do with major retailers wanting to buy a range of products by one company, or supermarket chains pushing their own home brand. 'They're driving manufacturers into obscurity,' says Mark Rowell. 'It takes all your identity away.'

Mention the Krisk Bean Slicer to Australians over 50, however, and they'll say 'Wasn't that the thing Joe the Gadget Man used to sell?' It was and, like many other kitchen gadgets at the time, a lot of selling was actually done. When Mark Rowell's father, Geoff, got involved with Tatham Cutlery in 1964, the factory was in a basement in Lee Street, near Central Station, and it was one person's job to go down to the fruit and vegetable markets in Chinatown, buy a stack of beans, and drop them into all the department stores in the city – McDowells, Hordern Brothers, Anthony Hordern, David Jones, Farmers, Marcus Clark. 'They'd have a little box in the kitchen department – you'd take out the beans from the day before, put the fresh ones in, and then customers could try out the bean slicer to see how well it worked.'

Mark Rowell says he gets letters 'all the time saying "I had the bean slicer and it's finally broken – it was my mother's and I got it 30 years ago, and it's good to see the Krisk's still around."' He even had someone drive 500 kilometres from Eden to Sydney to try and buy a new Krisk Bean Slicer. 'I said, "Hey, Lady, if you're going to drive from Eden, here's five dozen, take them away and give them to your friends."'

The Rowell family bought Tatham Cutlery after its founder, Bill Tatham, the inventor of the bean slicer, died. At the time, it was making only two things, the bean slicer and metal indicator hands – the manually operated type that shot out from the driver's window to indicate a right-hand turn. Geoff, who had been a buyer for David Jones in its London office for two years, had just come back to Australia, 'was at a loose end' and became manager of the new acquisition. 'I think Tatham Cutlery cost £6000 to buy,' he says. Not expensive, but probably overpriced as, six months later, legislation was introduced in favour of indicator lights. The hands, complete with their hand-painted nails and knuckles, became obsolete. That left the bean slicer – at the time, a metal gadget made in much the same way it had always been, which, to put it kindly, was makeshift.

Overall, the Krisk Bean Slicer is an ingenious thing, about the size of a vegetable peeler. It has a shielded blade at one end to top and tail the beans, and a hinged slot in the middle of the device to clamp the beans in place as they're dragged through a grille of six blades, the inner four to slice, the outer two to string the beans. Even when Geoff Rowell started with the company those blades were, incredibly, concocted from razor blades. 'You'd buy 200,000 razor blades at a time from England, and then sit down and break them up in a press – put one end in and snap the side off, snap the other side off and then snap it into little lengths.' There were 25 people in the factory just making Krisk Bean Slicers – and British exporters probably thinking Australian men were ridiculously clean shaven.

Now, eight people work in the factory, most of whom have been there for at least 10 years, and the blades come by the metre, rolled into large flat discs and chopped off as needed. These days the bean slicer itself is made of high-quality plastic, its parts automatically pumped out of injection-moulding machines. The blades are still laboriously fitted by hand, by two women who sit next to each other, slotting them in. You can see they've done it hundreds of thousands of times before, picking up the super-sharp fragments of metal as casually as if they were handling cardboard. Band-Aids, apparently, are the badges of novices. 'Women are better than men at doing it,' says Mark Rowell, whose wife, Alexandra, works in the office at Tatham Cutlery. 'Men have such big fingers, they're a bit bumbly when handling little things, and bumbly doesn't come into it. If something goes wrong and it falls apart, people will end up with razor blades in their food.' You have to care about making bean slicers, he says. 'You have to like making bean slicers to work here.' Geoff Rowell adds that they've looked many times at the possibility of the blade work being done by a robot, but it's too fiddly for that. There's a hand-written notice on one of the machines that says 600 bean slicers an hour is an acceptable number.

Geoff Rowell doesn't know much about Bill Tatham, the inventor of the Krisk Bean Slicer. 'I do know he used to ride around with his dog in a Rolls-Royce – whether that meant he made a lot of money out of all this, I don't know.' He possibly did – even

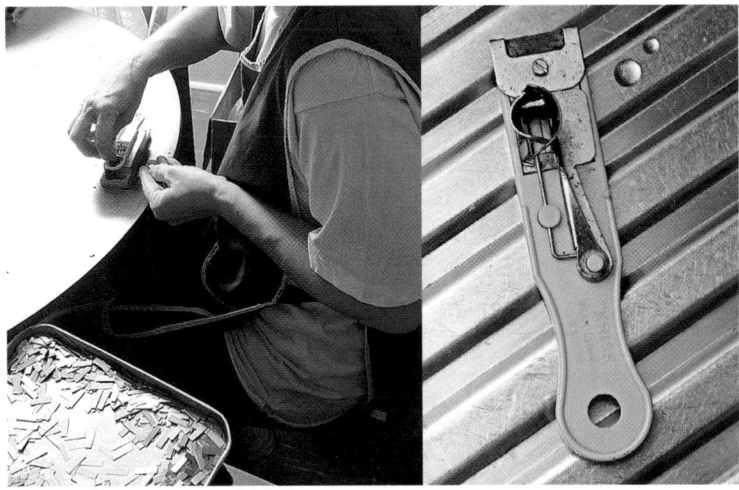

during the Second World War, the Krisk Bean Slicer kept being made, although it missed out on its chrome plating during those years. Looking through the company's historical documents, there's a cookery pamphlet when the gadget was first launched in which Krisk is turned into an adjective: 'Krisked Beans'. And there's a chart documenting the nutritional advantages of Krisked Beans over regular beans and other vegetables, 'explained by the even and correct cooking made possible by the uniform slicing of the vegetable, thus permitting all scientific changes to be regular'. The Rowells, 'of course', all use the Krisk Bean Slicer. According to Geoff Rowell, it makes the beans 'look better, cook better and taste better – that's what it used to say on the back of the packet. I'll tell you what, if we go to someone's place for dinner and they don't use the bean slicer, they're not beans. The bean slicer makes them look very presentable.'

As well as the bean slicer, the company originally made pocket knives and possibly other types of cutlery to justify the name. Geoff Rowell suspects the name Krisk is based on kris, the South-East Asian dagger. What he does know is that as soon as his family became involved in the company, it was clear they needed to start manufacturing something else. Even though the Krisk has always been the company's ‘bread and butter’, it’s not enough to keep a business going. For a while, it got involved in making aluminium saucepans, kettles and teapots, ‘but then aluminium got a very bad press, so we just closed that part of it down and walked away’.

The Krisk Bean Slicer is such a successful product that it gets copied – Mark Rowell pulls out the latest Chinese fake he’s come across – a flimsy-looking thing which, you imagine, could dispatch a whole lot of razor blades into a saucepan of beans. In the early days, patents were taken out, but now, he says, ‘on a thing like this, they’d be very expensive and cost you a lot to maintain. In the event of a copy, are you going to defend it in an international court – it’s hard to justify for a bean slicer.’

Tatham Cutlery now has very little to do with cutlery – it describes itself as a specialist in ‘plastic moulding and ultrasonic welding’, which sounds prosaic, but the products it manufactures, all for other people apart from the bean slicer, a knife sharpener and a gadget to julienne vegetables, make for an oddly interesting mix. Illuminated exit signs were partly developed by Tatham Cutlery and are made by the thousand at the factory. And then there are nit combs, ear plugs, flavoured mouthguards and compartmentalised boxes to hold a week’s worth of pills in breakfast, lunch and dinner order. Geoff Rowell helped streamline the design of the particular boxes the company manufactures, and also designed the packaging for many of the products. ‘I’m not an engineer, I’m not anything, but I’m a bit creative as far as these things are concerned.’ He also helped develop a kibbe mould, that makes 12 kibbe at a time instead of the usual one, and is now exported to Lebanon. Not so successful was a dog collar with a built-in lead. Geoff Rowell had no input into that design.

He is almost retired now, but can often be found upstairs at the factory, doodling with a pencil at a drawing board. ‘I’ve seen a few things that could have been done a bit better. There are that many potato peelers on the market, but I have an idea that I could do something a bit different.’

I can’t imagine what that would be, I say to him.

‘No, you can’t, and I’m not going to tell you.’

Cricket Bats

There are three arms to the Fisher cricket bat company. The farm in the southern Gippsland district of Victoria where 1500 willow trees grow. The workshop where the bats are made. The shop where the bats are sold, on a dreary expanse of Melbourne's Geelong Road at West Footscray, between a hairdresser and a grog shop. I meet Lachlan Fisher, who started the company about 16 years ago, at the shop, which has a small office and workroom at the back where you're likely to find him when there are no customers around. In the shop window and out the back in the workshop, neatly piled blocks of willow – some local and some imported from England, and traditionally house-shaped in profile – are drying out over several months until they're at the right stage to be worked on. Early in the conversation, Lachlan Fisher is talking about the processes involved in making a bat. 'We've got a workshop with all the tools – we machine the blocks of willow – we use electric planers, ripping saws…we use tungsten blades…and we have another big ripping saw for the logs…'

How many of you work here, I ask.

'Oh no, it's just me,' says Lachlan Fisher.

Lachlan Fisher *is* Fisher Cricket Bats & Willow – he grows the willow, he mans the machines between seven and eleven in the mornings in the workshop – which, it turns out, is behind his house – before he opens the shop. He spends Sunday mornings making cricket bats. He is what his accountant calls 'now, what is it he says…vertically integrated. It means we do every element.' He doubts there's anyone else in the world who does it all. Lachlan Fisher did employ someone to work in the shop for a while, but it was a waste of money. It wasn't that the bloke was no good – it was that anyone who came in to buy a Fisher bat wanted to know where the bat-maker was. He'd tell them Lachlan Fisher would be in on Friday. 'And then he'd tell me there were 10 people in that day and they'd be coming back on Friday. My Fridays were a nightmare.'

Every year he makes about 500 bats, most of which end up somewhere in Victoria, some in the hands of district players, others with schoolboys 'low down in the batting order who might only get a hit every three weeks'. A few Fisher bats make their way to New South Wales and to other states around Australia; others have been sold in England. The internet helps make this possible; there's no need for a sales rep to be out there spruiking the advantages of a Fisher bat.

Making bats was something Lachlan Fisher fell into. He'd trained as an artist, had a few exhibitions, taught at university, sold a few paintings, got some good reviews – 'My style was a combination of European figurative and Australian traditional…more a combination of Arthur Boyd, Sidney Nolan, Fred Williams' – got a Commonwealth grant to do a painting study of Lake Conder, near Warrnambool, where local Aborigines used elaborate fish traps to catch eel, but then he gave it away. 'We were poor – my wife's a singer and actor – and after a few years of painting, I thought there was no future financially. Melbourne's an expensive place to live, so I thought it was time to look for a serious job and paint between five and seven at night.' He worked for a while as a production manager in a graphic printing company before answering an ad for a job to set up a workshop repairing cricket bats with a view to making them. 'I started there and slowly taught myself how to hand-make bats, and how to deal with the machines and the willow.' Lachlan Fisher estimates he made about 5000 bats for that now-defunct company before starting his own business in 1993.

He's not a cricket fanatic, he says. 'I played cricket and still do, but not at a very high level.' And he watches it. 'I can find myself in the park, standing there for hours just watching it for no reason – I have no idea why.' But it's more the agricultural and manufacturing side of it that interests him. 'That's why we got involved in growing willow here – it came about because someone said it couldn't be done and I was determined to prove them wrong.' While most of the willow for his bats comes from England, he brought in genetic material from England 10 or 15 years ago to grow his own, which he now uses for his second brand, Ozblade. 'Sixteen years is the ideal length of time to grow willow,' he says. 'That means the grain definition, the lines on your cricket bat, are closer together. We can grow them a lot quicker than in England, but what the Poms are trying to do is have a slower growing tree which gives the high price.' The climate in southern Gippsland, he says, is as close as possible to that of Essex, where the timber for most of the English bats comes from.

Making and selling cricket bats is as seasonal as the game itself. The phone starts ringing in July, and by August he can be making up to 100 bats a month. I foolishly phoned him just before the cricket season started – he told me to ring back in a month. The lead-up to Christmas is busy, and then it starts dropping away, until it's almost dead by the end of June.

HANDMADE IN MELBOURNE AUSTRALIA
Fisher
Custom

Trees in southern Gippsland are felled in February 'so we still have enough heat to get a lot of moisture out of it'. Lachlan Fisher is a licensed tree feller – he felled trees in England when he was there on a Churchill Fellowship, studying tree-growing and cricket-bat making. 'I do all the splitting of logs, I load the trucks, do it all.' Shaped into blocks 28 inches long (everything in Lachlan Fisher's world is in imperial – the size of the saws, the width of the bats, everything) they're stacked in the shop for six months or more until they're ready for the next stage.

You can't help thinking about Stradivarius violins when Lachlan Fisher's talking about timber and bats and what makes a good bat. 'You can have a very very fast-growing tree that's quite dense and hard and equates to a lack of performance or you can have a very slow growing willow that's dense and hard and doesn't perform well. At the other end you get incredibly light, quite mythic performing bats and no one can work out why.' After making thousands of bats over the years, Lachlan Fisher can gauge a piece of timber almost as soon as he sees it, he says. He's after a piece that's 'light and furry' after it's been cut. 'When the saw's ripping down the grain and it comes off in stringiness or furriness, it means there's a lot of air in it, it's fibrous and it's got rebound.' He gauges timber by looking at it; Indian and Pakistani buyers, he says, usually give it a flick and listen to the pitch of it – a high note means it's dense, a low one 'that it's full, and if it's full of air it will play well – you need air in the willow for rebound'.

Timber's a fascinating, and frightening, material, says Lachlan Fisher. 'If we bring in 500 blocks of willow from England at great expense and make 500 bats, you have to accept that 20 per cent of them aren't going to be top end. It's scary when you're unpacking the blocks of willow and hoping you're going to get an 80 per cent strike rate, get your money back and make a profit.' Every block of timber you pick up is different he says. 'It's organic. All the hands-on operations with bat-making are non-prescriptive. You don't say "We're going to do this today, exactly." Every piece of timber has got to be pressed differently, for a start.'

Once the bat is cut into the basic shape, it's passed through a press, a simple roller that crushes the willow. Each piece of willow goes through the press about eight times, says Lachlan Fisher. 'That's an art in itself. A lot of people have presses pre-designed with weights. We don't do that because all willow's different and you can get into trouble if you've got willow that's a little bit hard. You can overpress it and it becomes harder. If you've got really lovely blocks of soft willow, sometimes you've got to overpress them so they don't get damaged. I do it by eye and feel, and look and watch the willow compacting and say "That's enough." When the blocks are wet, you get a feel for the sound, the noise as the water is squashed into the cells and squashed out the end.'

What you're trying to do, he says, is maximise the bat's potential – to make it commercial and match it with someone. 'If you adopt a very prescriptive approach, you'll get too many duds. You'll come out with an overmanufactured bat or an underdone one. It's a piece by piece process, especially with us. We're a boutique business. From pressing to hand-shaping is an evaluation of each block of wood. I've probably made 18,000 bats by hand and it takes the first 5000 to work out what to do, to ensure you don't make too many mistakes.'

Serious tools are used to make cricket bats – you could hurt yourself sending the raw logs through the ripping saw, 'a scary-looking thing with a 26-inch blade. We can't employ people to do it, it's a skill and it's dangerous. I have to do it myself.' Likewise the big curved draw knife, which 'we use to take all the weight off the back of the bat after it's been pressed'. Working out where to take the weight off is 'high skill to get it right, and thousands and thousands of bats to know what you're doing'. Even if someone doesn't play cricket, he says, they'll know a good bat when they pick one up. 'It's a human thing. It doesn't feel too heavy, doesn't feel too light. It feels good.' It's a bat, he says, with a 'big centre – the performance area of a cricket bat is about 7½ inches from the toe. That's your centre. Good bats, with a big centre, will hit the ball well from there to there,' he says stretching out his hand along the face of the bat. Shaping the bat, he says, can be one of the pleasures of the job. 'If you've got good willow, it's a joy, it feels like carving soap it comes off so easily.'

Other tools, some traditional English and Japanese ones which Lachlan Fisher estimates might be 150 years old – 'a little spoke shave, a flat plane and a rasp' – are used to work on the bat. You can see marks of the human hand on each one, specifically Lachlan Fisher's hand. 'All facets of the bat are handmade by me, I build style into the bat.' To harden the edges of a cricket bat, he used to use the traditional tool – a bone. Now he uses a stainless steel tool in the shape of one. 'It's still called boning the edges. Some of the old bat-makers used kangaroo bone, but it's absolutely useless. Fair dinkum, you had to cut the ends of the bone, put a thread through, and using two hands you'd put so much pressure on the bone that it would break. It was a waste of time – stainless steel is very heavy, doesn't stain the willow and has a lovely surface. There's traditional and there's commonsense.'

Lachlan Fisher reads a lot about the history of cricket and cricket bats. He talks about cricket bats in the 1770s being made out of single pieces of willow – not a very strong timber – and then, he says, makers started making the handles of a separate material. 'Originally the handles were of ash or some other material, which they would splice into the blade, but around the 1830s, the English were in South-East Asia, starting to farm, and discovered cane for furniture, and rubber. So in the 1830s, virtually all the bats had cane and rubber handles – English blades and handles from Sarawak. It's fascinating – you've got the two cultural aspects to a cricket bat.' The handles look just like pieces of cane – look carefully and inside are layers of rubber, which create the flex. Lachlan Fisher makes the handles if he has time, 'but we source most of the work out of India now – my labour costs are too high. They assemble the cane handles to our specifications and we turn them here on the lathe, and splice them, which is cutting the V to slot them into the blade. There's more work in making a handle than in finishing a bat, much more work.'

Lachlan Fisher is pragmatic about making cricket bats. When I ask if there's anything creative about it, he says there is at times, in the retailing and strategy and crafting. It's not the same as in painting, though. 'You can lose yourself in a piece of art and wake up and wonder where you've been for the past two hours. This is a totally different thing. The phone rings halfway through a cricket bat and it doesn't matter.'

RODDY
MED-SMALL
LEGS

'Must've been one sick little puppy who did that.'

Geoff Chapman is looking at the crime scene-like photo of the injuries. Multiple stab wounds. Injuries to the chest, stomach and face. Guts spilling out. Eyes just about done for. Jealous lover, apparently, says Geoff Chapman.

The way he tells it, the couple has a fight – she goes out to cool down a bit. Comes home and goes berserk when she finds her great big fat sandy coloured teddy bear, a present from – naturally – a previous boyfriend, lying there with stuffing oozing out all over the place.

Potentially fatal injuries, but the specialists at Sydney's Doll Hospital do a brilliant job of microsurgery. You can hardly see a scar in the post-op shots. 'Don't know if the relationship survived,' says Geoff Chapman. 'I'd be getting away from him if I were her.'

The Doll Hospital isn't qualified to do couples counselling, but can tackle just about any injury to dolls of all ages, teddy bears, china dogs or, it seems from what's up in the workshop, pretty well any well-loved ornament or decorative item around the house, as well as suitcases, handbags, umbrellas and dolls' prams.

To get to the workshop, you have to make your way through the shop, an overwhelmingly kitsch cavern jammed with frills and glitz, saccharine and lace. The kinds of dolls grown women buy, apparently – a million miles from the faded sweetness of the dolls I remember from childhood.

But through a curtain and up the stairs out the back, the atmosphere changes – the shininess and unappealing perfection of the shop makes way for something altogether darker and more interesting – there's dust and grime and hospital green paint; the claustrophobia of the massed overdressed is replaced by an expanse sprawling with body parts. There's something thrillingly creepy about it, which Geoff Chapman can't see. 'I suppose I've known it all my life – they're just dolls to me. Some people reckon they wouldn't want to be up here on their own of a night though.'

It's too ordered to be the work of a suicide bomber. Chubby little arms, many of them grubby, are piled up in a pyramid shape on a table at the top of the stairs. In front of a window, arms, legs and a torso – all from the same body – are pegged to a line. Torsos hang from hooks. In one corner of the room, jam jars hold the remnants of various shades of flesh-toned paint. Disembodied heads with vague expressions, all facing in the same direction, are lined up on shelves.

The space is broken up with a massive makeshift divider, reaching up to the ceiling – tea chests on their sides, opening to the front, six high and 24 along. It looks as if it was made when the the Doll Hospital moved into the building 40 years ago. On the other side, it's the same deal. Pegboard and chipboard panels, tacked to the fronts of the tea chests, make sure their contents don't spill out. Italian Legs, Italian Arms, Medium Vinyl Heads, Bent Pedigree Legs, say some of the signs. From one, all you can see sticking up over the chipboard barrier are the soles of a pair of little feet. Doll Cemetery says a sign hanging on one of the tea chests. We Hate Barbie, someone has scrawled in black underneath. Poke around the open shelving in one part of the space and there are layers and layers of sheets of foam plastic, studded with rows of holes, each the size to hold an eyelashed eye. A sheet of blue eyes, a sheet of brown and

on it goes. Pick up a sheet and the eyes – all but one or two lazy ones – blink open alarmingly in unison. Underneath are a whole load of 'mama voices' – plastic cylinders that sound like cows when turned upside down. On nearby shelves are minority doll parts – all black, and in cardboard boxes with signs saying things like Black Pedigree Cherub Heads.

The saddest two tea chests are full of boys' heads – so few among the millions of dolls, and every single one of them looks slightly gormless, unlike the lively girls around them. A row of absolutely identical heads on a shelf nearby has a whiff of Dolly the Sheep. Opposite, a wall is lined with dozens of boxes of suitcase handles and locks.

The handles and locks are a reminder of the way the Doll Hospital has changed over the years. It started out, more than 90 years ago, by accident – the result of what's gone down in history as the 1917 general strike in New South Wales. The strike was over the railway management's introduction of card systems, designed to record how much work everyone was doing. Not that that matters here – the main thing is that Harold Graham Chapman, a railway boilermaker in Sydney, was out of work. His brother Archibald owned the American Bag Stores, a string of bag shops across the city. Along with bags, he sold celluloid dolls from Japan. After several weeks on an un-air-conditioned ship through the tropics, the elastic which kept heads, limbs and torsos intact would snap and the wooden cases would be a jumble of body parts. 'Somehow my grandfather taught himself to re-elastic the dolls,' says Geoff Chapman.

All went smoothly until Archibald said that monkeys could be taught to do the job. Harold Graham Chapman stormed off and went into business for himself, repairing dolls and selling Chinese napery out of a general store in the Sydney suburb of Campsie. Being a boilermaker, he was handy and worked out how to repair all sorts of dolls, but what his mates on the railways thought of his new career, it's impossible to say.

Over time, he built up a good business, also acting as an agent for doll repairs from toy shops all over the place. During the Thirties, by which time Geoff Chapman's father, also called Harold, was involved in the company, the Doll Hospital moved into Her Majesty's Arcade in the centre of the city.

When the Second World War broke out, it was impossible to get linen supplies in from Asia, but that was not a problem for the business. 'In many ways, it was boom time,' says Geoff Chapman. With higher national priorities, dolls weren't being imported into Australia, and manufacturing of such non-essentials was severely restricted. 'Mums and dads couldn't buy new dolls for Christmas, so they'd get the old one repaired or buy a new dress for it – that's what would happen.'

That was hardly the basis for a wildly successful business, and so the Chapmans diversified. 'They'd repair everything you could think of,' says Geoff Chapman. Nylon stockings for a start. 'How the hell would you work out how to repair nylon stockings – I have no idea.' But they experimented, and found people with all sorts of expertise – at its peak there were 70 employees spread over six studios repairing suitcases, handbags, umbrellas, ladies' gloves, toys and anything else that crossed their worktables. Geoff Chapman remembers that some of the experts were a bit strange. 'There was one little old lady who used to repair the teddy bears. She lived in a convent for some reason, and always used to talk to the teddy bears while she was working on them. I have no idea what she was saying.'

Many of the methods and materials those workers developed to repair dolls are still used today – the simple tools, the liquid forms of celluloid and hard plastic – although tremendous advances in glues and epoxies have made life easier.

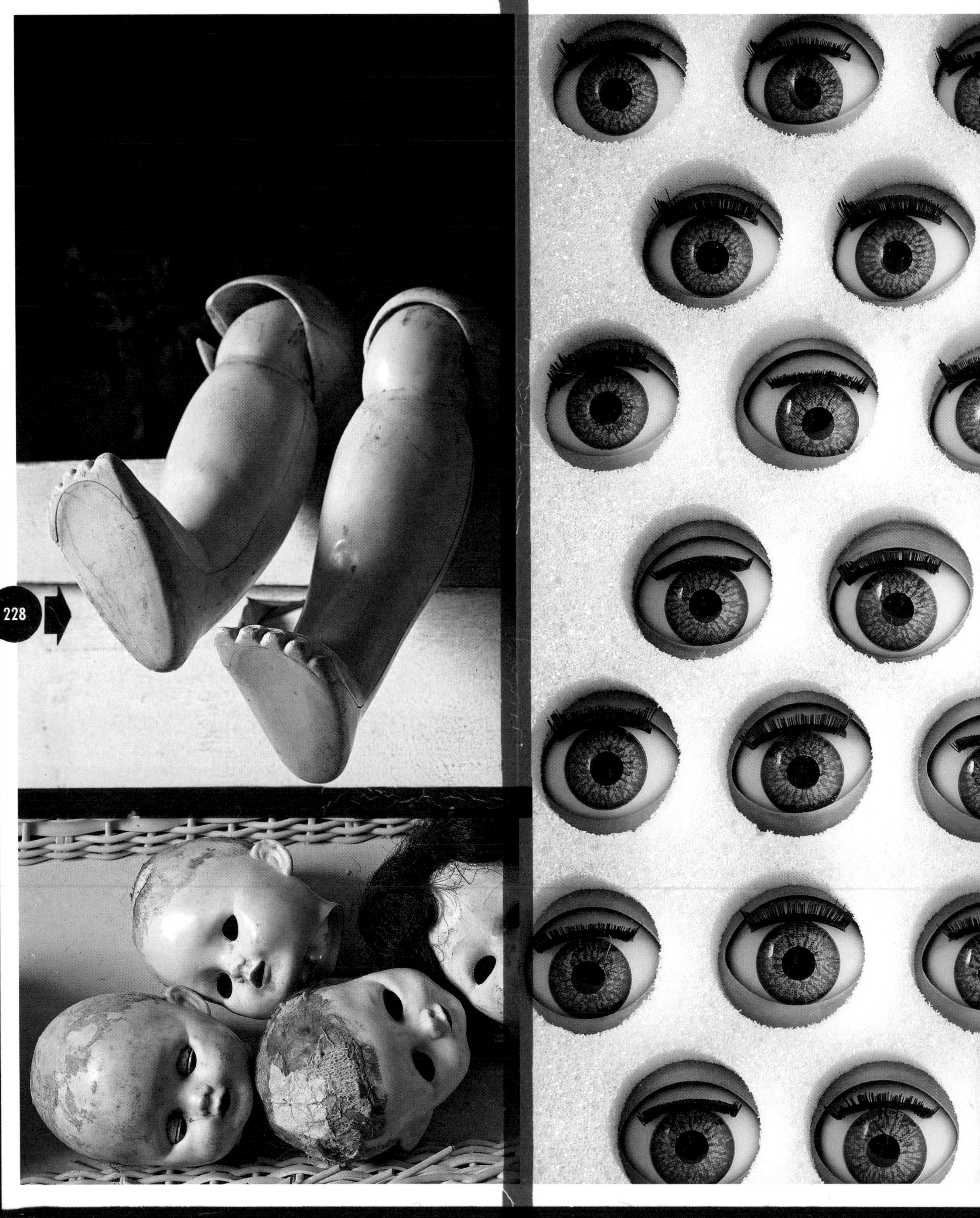

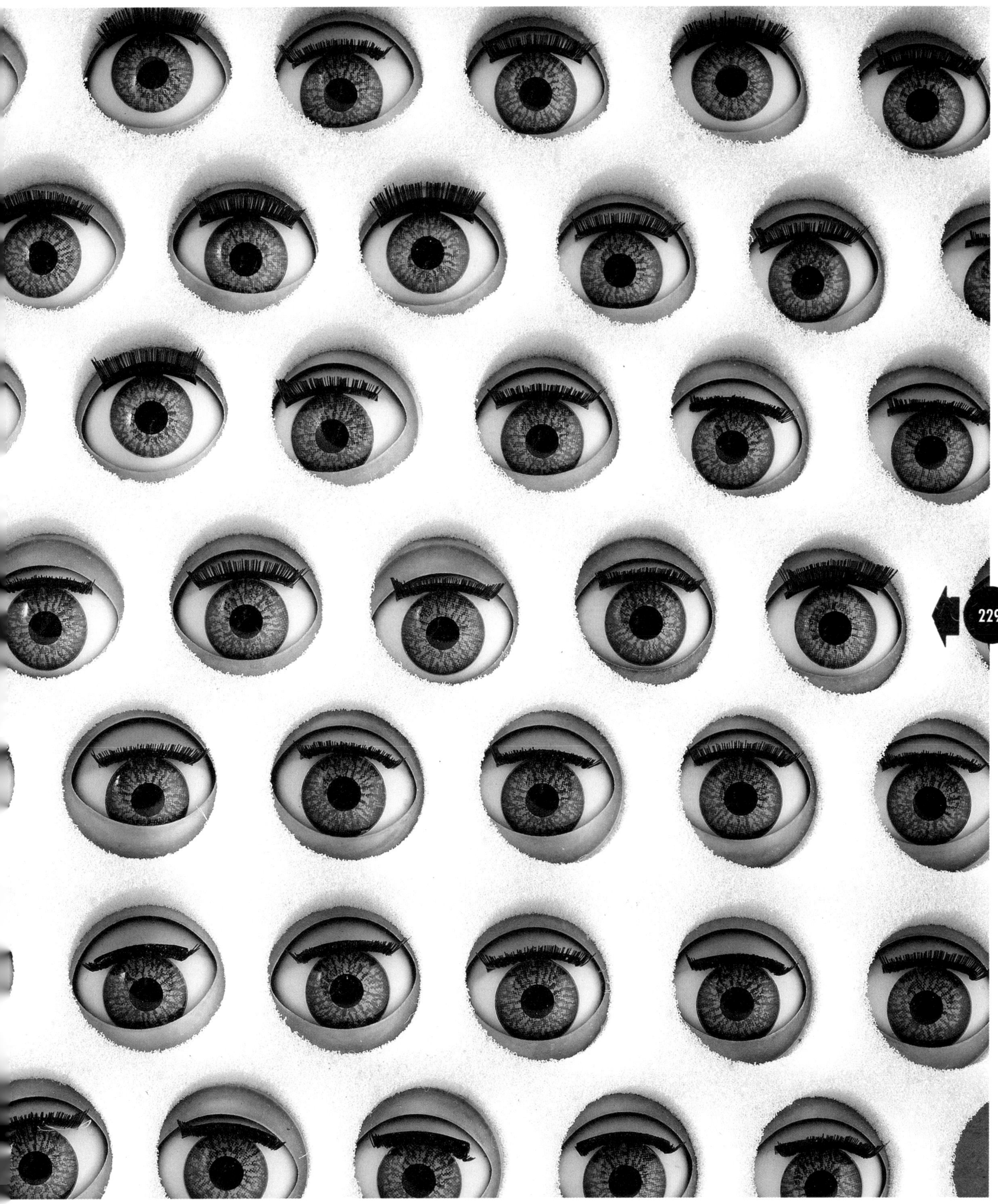

After the war, the company also went into thermoplastics – they saw the 'future as plastic moulding' and also recognised it as a handy way of manufacturing spare parts for dolls. So along with arms and legs, they were making saucepan handles and doing other contract work, 'making anything that anyone wanted moulded' – it didn't turn out to be quite the flourishing business they were hoping for, but many of those little arms and legs piled up in tea chests in the Bexley workshop are from those days.

In 1968, when Her Majesty's Arcade was knocked down to make way for Centrepoint shopping centre and tower, the Doll Hospital had to move from its inner-city location. It set up shop in Bexley, where it is now, and Geoff Chapman, who'd done a management traineeship with retailer G. J. Coles as an express way of learning skills for the family company, joined the business. He'd worked in the shop doing odd jobs during school holidays and there was never really any discussion that he'd do anything else with his life. He's always liked toys, he says, and did run a chain of toy shops for a while. As for dolls and teddies, one of the Chapman family stories involves him, at the age of about seven, asking his father about a teddy sitting in a corner of the Doll Hospital. 'He gave me a heart-wrenching story about a little girl who'd lost it. It was a dirty-looking old thing, but I insisted on taking it home. My father cursed me – I could have had any toy I'd wanted – but it was there in my room for ages. I just felt sorry for it.'

He doesn't often see that attachment to dolls and teddy bears by the current generation of children. 'Oh, you see it every now and then, and it's nice. You know what it can be like – the kid can't go to bed without the doll or teddy bear, which can make it awkward if it needs repairing. We'll drop everything to get it back as quickly as we can – if it's only an eye missing, we'll do it in a day, but sometimes things take much longer.'

These days, it's more 'the big people' who get attached to their dolls. 'A lot of them do get very emotional when they bring them in, and then when they come in again to pick them up.' He's not as diplomatic as he could be, he says. 'I've often had the situation where someone's brought in a doll or teddy bear and asked me if it could be repaired. I'll look and say it's not worth doing and some of them get very annoyed. They say "I didn't ask you whether it was worth it, I asked you if you could do it."' One of the few remaining dolls' hospitals in the world, they have even had dolls sent to them from the United States.

Missing eyes are some of the most common injuries – mainly from curious kids who give a poke to work out how the sleeping eye works. Enthusiastic, but not promising, hairdressers are also a menace; replacing dolls' hair is part of the routine work at the Doll Hospital. Missing fingers are another regularly seen injury, and replacing them is no problem at all to the specialist team, each of whom work on different types of dolls.

One of the greatest hazards for dolls and bears, says Geoff Chapman, is the family mutt. 'Dogs get very jealous, and the bears and dolls bear the brunt of it. They see the owner cuddling the teddy and that's it – it'll be ripped to pieces.' They're not the only problem, though. A quick flick through an album of before and after pictures shows the range of injuries. One note attached to a mangled doll with round glasses, a beard and eyebrows drawn on, reads, 'My next door neighbour's child drew all over my little girl's baby doll with black texta – when her brother tried to stop him doing it, he broke the doll's arm.' The baby looked perfectly healthy in the after photo.

These days, the Doll Hospital only has four workers on the premises, and that includes Geoff Chapman. Some of the work is farmed out to local experts – an automotive specialist, for instance, works on the undercarriages of prams, a cane worker repairs the wicker.

The day we're visiting, a woman comes into the shop with a skinny, filthy teddy bear – a cheap-looking thing, the sort you'd pick up in an amusement arcade. It would cost about $300 to fatten it up with stuffing and clean it, she's told. No guarantees on the cleaning front – its coat is clearly inferior.

'Not worth doing,' she says. 'Do you think I should take it to the dry cleaners – would that do any good? Could they clean it?'

Geoff Chapman stays calm and tells her it would make it worse, that it wouldn't survive the chemicals. His assistant is holding the teddy carefully in her arms, as if it has broken bones. She hands it back to the customer, who takes the creature away with her. This is one that's probably not going to make it.

Carriage Maker and Wheelwright

It's an odd place to be hearing the history of the wheel – in a workshop in Adelaide, not far from the airport. But on a wet autumn morning Peter Foster tells at least part of the story – backwards and forwards, shifting from continent to continent. Centuries, millennia, kilometres disappear as he talks about Cobb & Co coaches, Assyria, Henry Ford, Napoleon, mediaeval England, rice paddy carts, Wells Fargo. There's no room here for cartoon images of Stone Age wheels; he dates the 'oldest, most significant invention', the wheel, back, most probably, to ancient Egypt.

Peter Foster is a carriage maker and wheelwright. In the old days, he says, wheelwrights were generally well-educated, well-read characters. 'Don't ask me why, maybe it's because of the complexity of the business, the damned time it takes. They were patient people.' He talks about Americans simplifying the process of making a wheel and introducing production-line methods, killing off the wheelwright trade in a space of five years. He sees strong parallels between the demise of the horse-drawn

vehicle and the current crisis in the automotive industry. 'We've gone potty over a whole age of motor cars, but the whole thing started 100 years before. All we did was put motors in what they already had.'

A wheel, he says, can take a week or two to make when all the work's done by hand, using such tools as a spoke shave and draw knives, many of which he's bought in antique shops. 'Sometimes nothing goes right and it slows you down.' As he takes us on a tour of the wheel, it's clearly a very complicated piece of engineering with its wooden hub, crafted to hold the teardrop-shaped spokes (which are found only on 'finely built vehicles' in contrast to the easier-to-make round spokes) and each fitted individually, 'like fitting a shoe'; and the arc-shaped timber fellies, or segments of the rim, which all fit together, jigsaw-like and keep the spokes in place. Around many of the old wheels, a steel tyre, heated to black-hot so it's big enough to slip over the wooden components ('not red-hot otherwise it would burn the timber'), keeps all elements in place. 'As soon as you put it on, you get your watering can or hose and cool it to shrink it. It's that shrinking that tightens up all the joints on the wheel and holds it all together.' Once the tyre goes, he says, the whole wheel falls to bits.

American hickory, says Peter Foster, was traditionally used to make wheels. Axe handles and hammer handles were made of the same timber. 'It has a memory – if you belt the axe into a great lump of timber, the handle flexes and comes back again. It doesn't split, it doesn't crack. If the wheel hits a rut, it does a bit of a wobble and a squeak but rights itself and off it goes.' Australian wheelwrights found some of the local timbers worked just as well – blackwood, wandoo, river red gum. The English had to make do with elm or ash, 'the best they had but it wasn't good, it split – their roads were better, though, which made it a lot easier for coaches'.

Peter Foster learnt to make wheels by reading old trade journals, 'by doing a lot of thinking, and a lot of asking people. The old chaps I found who made wheels – there weren't many – they told me little shortcuts, the things you don't find in books. It's like today – if you came back in 100 years and read about how to work with a computer, do you think it would say you have to turn it on? Everyone would assume you knew that, it's those little assumptions that were the key to what I needed to know.'

When we visit his workshop, Peter Foster is working on a set of wheels for an 1858 Irish hearse. He'll be working on the body of the hearse later. You wonder how an Irish hearse ends up in Australia. 'I think, how does anything get here,' he says. This one wasn't such a mystery – an Australian collector bought it in England 50 years ago and shipped it back.

In his workshop, there are a number of pieces waiting for restoration – an 1840s boneshaker of a bicycle – 'I've had devil's strife with it because the jolly thing was all twisted in the frame' – an Edwardian ice cream cart with a serving bench all the way round, a stripy canvas roof, a pair of shafts for the pony.

In one way or another, Peter Foster has been working with wheels and carriages for the past 30 years or so. His father was a farrier. 'He was a horseman and anything to do with horses he could do. He used to show horses and ship horses off to India.' When the Indian trade dried up in the mid-Fifties, he got involved with trotting and transporting horses; after he semi-retired in the Seventies, he started showing harness. He bought a couple of horse-drawn vehicles, and Peter Foster got involved in cleaning them up and getting them ready for showing. The carriages he cleaned up then were 'slightly over-restored in order to be flashy, showy – over the top in order to be noticed'. You didn't worry too much about whether the work was authentic or not, he says.

His work was noticed; after he'd finished restoring a couple of sulkies for his father, he was commissioned by other people. At the time, he'd trained as a coach-painter and sign-writer. The people who trained him were, themselves, trained in the 1900s, and had been trained by people who'd worked in the late part of the nineteenth century. 'What they were giving me and what I was observing, although I didn't realise it at the time, was all the stuff I needed for what I do now.' On and off, he also taught carpentry at TAFE, trained at university to become an art teacher, and worked in graphic design for a while. He's also worked in display for a department store, and painted backdrops for a theatre company; all skills, too, he says, which he can put to use, one way or another, now.

It was partly his university art training, along with, perhaps, the wisdom of years, that led Peter Foster to change his attitude towards restoring horse-drawn vehicles. He'd rather an original piece, less than perfect, is left in place, than be replaced with something gleaming and new. He'd rather hand-paint 17 layers of paint, and rub down between each coat, than approach anything with a spray-gun. 'Spray-guns don't come into it; spray-painting doesn't penetrate the timber, there's no great sense of adhesion. It doesn't have the life of hand-painted stuff, it doesn't have the appearance, but more important to me, it's not authentic.'

A spoke on one of the hearse wheels snapped when he went to pull it out; he had tried to keep all the old ones, but sometimes that's not possible. And anyway, he says, when it comes to wheels, what's original? 'Wheels are the equivalent of the bases of long-case clocks. You get Georgian long-case clocks, and very rarely is the bottom bit original. The clocks all sat on stone, everyone swooshed the floor with water, so the bottom bits rotted out.'

Everything Peter Foster does takes time. There are very few individuals, he says, willing to pay for that. Most of his business comes through museums, government departments, organisations such as the National Trust, and some large companies. He's restored about 30 vehicles for the National Trust in Millicent, South Australia. 'The best collection in Australia, the whole gamut – a governor's car, rustic carts, bakers' carts, landaus, broughams…' He restores the wheels on trophy guns – artillery pieces captured by the allies during wartime, shipped back to Australia and used as monuments in schoolyards and council parks. 'They always need new wheels – leaving them out in the weather is a bad thing for a wheel, it's a bad thing for everything.'

And out in the weather, he says, is where most wagons, coaches and other horse-drawn vehicles end up. 'People think it's a great idea to add some rusticity to their property by pulling up a wagon and watching it fall to bits, while people like me are busy trying to preserve the thing.' He talks, too, about Lord Byron's coach, which turned up in Port Lincoln, on South Australia's Eyre Peninsula, a town best known for tuna fishing. 'It lived there for 40 years, came out with his girlfriend,' he says. 'He gave her his best coach and sent her on her way. It ended up with a hotelkeeper – people used to come in and ask to have a bit of Lord Byron's coach and go and cut a piece off. *Cut it up*. Isn't that incredibly Australian.'

Peter Foster talks about his father being a nineteenth century man living in the twentieth century. It's hard not to feel the same way about him – living in the wrong century, living in the wrong place, dealing with the wrong people. His first trip to Europe was a few years ago, when he was 60. 'There's a book by a bloke, Colin Simpson, called *Wake Up In Europe*. By hell, don't you. By the living hell, don't you

wake up in Europe. The minute I walked into the Schönbrunn Wagenhaus in Vienna, by golly I did some learning. There was a whole load of stuff there that no beggar had tampered with, had wrecked. It had been preserved by people who knew what the hell they were doing. The great thing about that collection is it's run by the art department of the Historisches Museum, by the people who look after the Rubens and the Caravaggios.'

A couple of years ago Peter Foster restored a carousel, built in the late nineteenth century by 'Tidman's in Norfolk' and using German horses. The English liked German horses, he says, because they had 'a galloping motion, like an old painting'. It came out to Australia from the UK in the early twentieth century, and travelled around Victoria before settling in Adelaide, only moving between the funfair at the beachside suburb of Glenelg and the Adelaide Show. 'It has the most wonderful original set of horses on it, pretty much its original steam engine…but like all fairground things, it had suffered from years of fairground paint. Every Joe that's a hand on the fairground gets the job of painting, and they do it with a six-inch brush that's never been cleaned.'

A carpentry team had worked on it and removed the pressed metal and glass 'bohemian jewels', as they're called, from the saddles and bridles. Peter Foster tracked some down, and had copies made. In the Forties, a screen showing Robert the Bruce and Boadicea was painted over with portraits of generals and air vice-marshals from the Second World War, heroes of the then owner. One panel shows the Queen.

It was the middle of the school holidays when we visited the Beach House at Glenelg where the carousel is now permanently in place, under cover, alongside amusement arcade video games and fast food joints. There are queues to get on the horses. Digital cameras flash as children, some terrified, take their rides. The bohemian jewels glint under the lights. The top of the carousel is decorated with panels of busty Art Nouveau nymphs, clothed only in gauze. The paintings of military men, middle-aged and in uniform, look oddly formal, sitting at desks behind the perpetual motion of outstretched horses.

FRILL
$60

Umbrellas

Alicia Mora-Hyde often gets caught in the rain with no umbrella. Soaked, and hair dripping. With global warming, rain may not be as predictable as it used to be, but you'd think Alicia Mora-Hyde would always have an umbrella on her. She makes the things. Thousands of them. Folding umbrellas, men's umbrellas, brides' lacy numbers, beach umbrellas that look as if they belong in the south of France, standard umbrellas, parasols, double umbrellas plain on the outside, opening to a riot of colour in the lining. They're all there in the Brisbane factory of Mora-Igra Umbrellas.

It's a factory filled with rows and rows of deep shelves of half-made umbrellas, fully made umbrellas, umbrella frames, umbrella shafts, bolts of fabric, rolls of brown paper for drawing up the patterns, handles by the thousand (dogs' heads and some intricately carved; sensible-looking wooden ones and delicate mother-of-pearl coloured handles, any type of handle you can imagine); cabinets full of tassels and trims, braid and cord; boxes full of fabric, cut out, ready to stitch into umbrellas. Then there are the machines, each designed for a specific part of the umbrella-making process – machines that have been used for half a century or more; a couple look like sewing machines, another, for cutting from patterns, looks like a chainsaw. In her office at the front of the factory, chests of drawers are filled with umbrellas – 'too many' different types, altogether, too many to count.

As far as Alicia Mora-Hyde knows, she's the last person left in Australia making umbrellas. There used to be at least one umbrella company in every city, but with $5 throwaways and status symbol imports, there's not such a demand for the locally made version. Even if it is made of gold lamé or lined with Liberty lawn, as some of Alicia Mora-Hyde's are. 'My umbrellas are not for rain, they're about beauty,' she says. 'People don't buy them when it's raining, they buy them when they want something different.' Some of them do buy them for rain as well, I'm sure, although when I rang later, after a week of Queensland rain, business had been particularly slow.

Alicia Mora-Hyde's story – what she'll tell of it – is a migrant's tale. There are hundreds of other stories like it in Australia. 'Miserable, unhappiness and everything else' is the reason she came to Australia. She won't give away every detail because she's determined to write her own book one day, but it goes something like this. She was born on a farm in Chile, one of 13 children. 'My mother and father are cat and dog – they never ever got on but that's beside the point.' Her father was difficult, she says, 'and I didn't get on with my mother, I never did. She's still alive. I love her dear.'

She ran away from home at 17, and worked in a clothes shop in the city, 'and went to school at night because I didn't have high school, only the first six years'.

Alicia Mora-Hyde was content there, but 'I said to myself "This shop will close one day and I'll have nothing to do."' The solution, she decided, was to move to another country. The idea was to work in America for a few years and then go back to Chile and open her own shop. 'But a lady I knew said it was very easy to come to Australia, they even give you the ticket. It was true, they did give me the ticket, and I just wanted to go anywhere.'

There was nothing adventurous about it, she says, even though she didn't know anyone in Australia. 'Everyone thinks it's so daring, but it's simple, I just packed my things, that's it.'

When Alicia Mora-Hyde arrived in Sydney, she couldn't speak much English, and could only get manual work. 'It was in a chocolate factory but I wasn't good for nothing, so they sacked me. I was probably too unhappy – they sacked all the girls.'

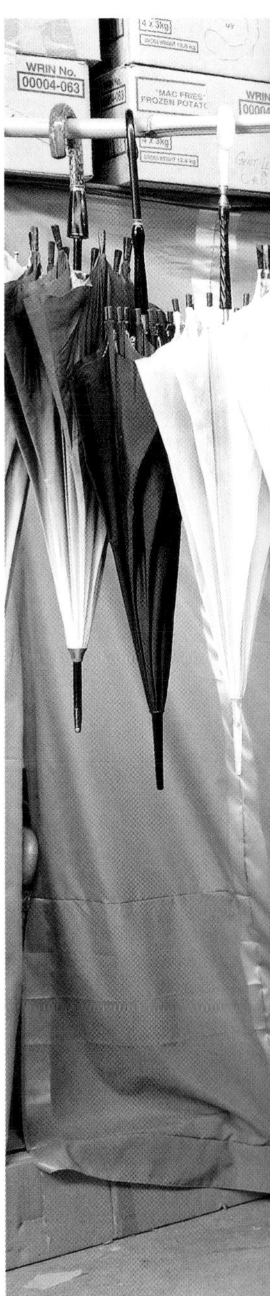

Contents

$ 40

FRILL
$60

FRiLL
$60

In 1971 she became a nanny to two young boys who lived with their father, 'a filthy rich man, the most beautiful businessman'. He owned an umbrella factory that had been going since 1948 in the centre of Sydney. It employed 20 or 30 people, and sold umbrellas all over Australia.

Once the boys were old enough to go to school, Alicia Mora-Hyde stayed on in the house. 'I didn't know where else to go,' she says. 'He was a good man, I lived with him for 30 years. I didn't *live* with him, I was never his lover. He didn't think of me like that. I was very skinny when I came to him, I had long hair, I was a migrant. I liked him very much.'

After having jobs in the post office for a couple of years at Christmas-time, she started working in the umbrella factory. 'I liked it from the start as a matter of fact. So many cloths, so many materials, so many colours. I just warmed to umbrellas, I suppose. I'm not a reader, I like classical music, but I'm not sure who plays. All my life I've liked classical music and it's the same with umbrellas. For me to work with umbrellas is a joy, I don't know what to say.'

Alicia Mora-Hyde eventually became the floor manager at the umbrella factory. 'Little by little I was learning it all.' Unlike everyone else there, who knew their own section, but nothing else. 'The one who puts the tips on, she doesn't even have to open her eyes to do it, like when you touch-type. You make the frame, you cut an umbrella, sew an umbrella, put the tips on, put it in the frame, tie it in, make the stud and at the end send it to the tailor who puts the handle on. I do it all now. I went from one section to another being the manager.'

She reckons she's the only woman in the world who can make an umbrella from start to finish. And it always was women who made umbrellas, she says. 'If a woman makes an umbrella, she'll still get her husband to do the handle. That's a man's job, it's too hard for a woman. That's why we used to send it to the tailor. Making a frame is not for a woman either.' The frame, from Germany or England, comes in multiple pieces – putting it together is like solving an intricate puzzle. The first telescopic umbrella frame ('very, very hard') Alicia Mora-Hyde ever made was perfect, except it was upside down, with the ribbed section opening beyond the shaft. 'It would make a good umbrella for a dog,' she says, miming a demonstration of walking with lead in one hand, umbrella pointed downwards, over an imaginary dog, probably a poodle.

As well as making umbrellas, Alicia Mora-Hyde used to visit department stores selling them, working with buyers to create colour combinations. 'I don't make for myself, I make for the public,' she says. 'I see a person and I know immediately what a person likes and dislikes. Maybe somebody loves orange like I love navy or light blue. I couldn't go out with an orange umbrella. I did an umbrella in Sydney – green inside and heavy orange outside. Horrible colours. I said to the girl beside me "We're going to make this and someone will love it." A lady from Belarus bought it.'

Alicia Mora-Hyde isn't telling much more of the Sydney story, but, almost 30 years after she started in the factory, the owner died. Before his death, 'he wanted to give the business to his sons', she says. 'They didn't want it, and then he wanted to give it to a nephew, another nephew, never me. He'd said "What's the point of giving it to you when you have no idea – if I say it's all yours, what would you do with it?" I told him I'd learnt the whole trade, no one else could do it.' One of the reasons she wanted the company, she says, 'is I thought one day the children will come. There must be some umbrellas genes there, but it doesn't look like it at the moment.'

When she took over the business, Alicia Mora-Hyde couldn't stay in Sydney. Semi-industrial buildings were becoming increasingly difficult to come by, and rents were ridiculous. And so in 2002, by then in her early sixties, she moved to Brisbane. 'Just another move' is the way she describes it – the fact that she knew no one in the Queensland capital was irrelevant. Soon after she moved there, she met a man at a birthday party, and within three months was married. 'He had a beautiful factory, too, once upon a time, here in Brisbane. He made cranes. I love him dearly.'

The warehouse she works out of now houses all the stock and machinery from the old factory – 'I haven't had to buy anything except a little bit of fabric – I buy some from Spotlight, some from the Salvation Army and St Vincent de Paul, and also from Chile' – and where, once, a couple of dozen women worked in the factory, now Alicia Mora-Hyde does it by herself. She makes umbrellas and also repairs them. She shows us a 100-year-old umbrella she's repairing – she removes the old fabric, using it to make a pattern for the new fabric and puts it back together again. It should last another 100 years, she says.

She couldn't say how many umbrellas she can make in a day, 'because I don't make them one by one. When I get sick and tired of one thing, I do something else. If my back is hurting I do something else.' The hardest umbrellas to make, she says, are

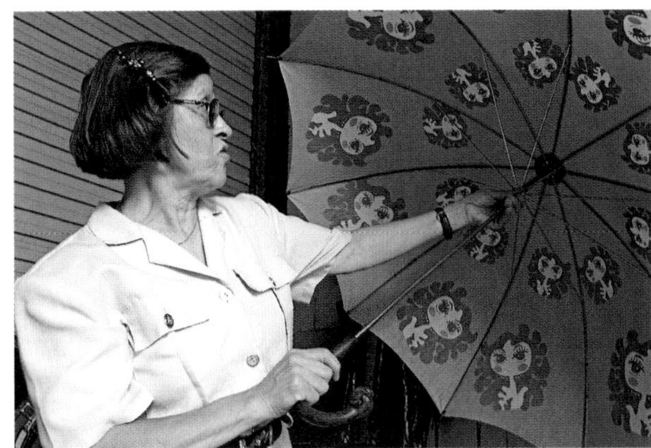

the lace ones and those of very flimsy material – you have to be careful with them. If she was younger, had more energy and didn't have so many umbrellas to sell, she says, she'd make 'dresses with umbrellas – children's dresses with matching umbrellas. I want to make umbrellas with Australian designs, too – one or two patterns with a kookaburra and a kangaroo. It would be a tourist thing.'

Alicia Mora-Hyde only sells umbrellas from her factory – she doesn't try to sell to shops. 'Big shops don't want me – they don't know me, they don't want my umbrellas.'

She'd like to pass her skills on to someone else 'but I don't know anyone who'd want to learn. I'm 67 now – I don't know how long I'll be working. I love the umbrellas as much as I love my husband. My mind wants to be here forever because I love making umbrellas, but my body doesn't want to bring me to this place, my body wants to stay in bed the whole day.'

This is a trade, says Alicia Mora-Hyde, 'that will be gone with the wind one day and that's very sad'.

Manufacturing Silversmith

W. J. Sanders is at the back of an industrial lot in Sydney's Marrickville. The way in is via one small door, usually closed. Inside, along one wall are shelves and shelves of old metal boxes – some close to a century old – with white, very obviously hand-painted labels identifying each. Chalice. Child's mugs. Bishop's Candlestick. Ciborium. Open a box and inside are drawstring calico bags, each containing several handmade wooden 'chucks', as they're called – the patterns for making the chalices, candlesticks and ciboria. Stack up the small wooden pieces by hand, like a child's toy, and you get an idea of the shape of the finished object. On top of the shelves are huge chucks – too big to fit inside boxes, beautiful in their own right, the layers of timber clearly visible, the smooth curves something you want to run your hands over.

The placement of these items, just inside the front door, isn't accidental. Dennis de Muth, who bought W. J. Sanders in 1996, used to be in marketing with Rémy Martin. 'Working for a French company, I understood the value of heritage, of history. I wanted to make it obvious straightaway how important history was here.'

As far as Australian manufacturing companies go, W. J. Sanders is well documented, with silverware by the company in Sydney's Powerhouse Museum, a detailed history of the company written and published. Dennis de Muth hadn't been planning to buy W. J. Sanders. A year earlier, he and wife Claire had bought Church Stores, and the manufacturing silversmith was their supplier for collection plates, lecterns and other religious metalware. The owners rang one day to tell them they were closing down. 'I said they couldn't, it was too important. If they went, these skills would be lost forever.'

Along with the company, the only surviving manufacturing silversmith in Australia, he took possession of all its intellectual property – the old design books, the old tools, the old chucks, everything. 'If I hadn't been able to get that, the deal wouldn't have happened.'

The company was started by William James Sanders, an Englishman, who trained in silversmithing in Birmingham before arriving in Sydney in 1911. Most of his early business came in the form of repair and restoration work. The First World War changed that – shipments of silverware stopped coming into the country for a few years, and jewellery houses and wholesalers started looking around to see if any local manufacturers could fill the gap. And so William James Sanders started making silverware – small items, popular at the time, such as napkin rings, cigarette cases, photo frames and powder compacts, as well as sporting trophies, including the 18-carat gold Sydney Cup for horseracing in the early 1920s. Later on, he made trophies for boxing, rifle shooting, yachting, golfing, athletics and other sports.

Leading up to the Second World War, he became more ambitious, his output broadening to include tea and coffee services, silver salvers, tankards, christening mugs and sauceboats. Many were designed and manufactured for major jewellers, such as Hardy Bros., Fairfax and Roberts, and Prouds. After Sanders died in 1946, control of the company passed to his widow, Ellen, with son John joining soon after.

With the enormous influx of migrants after the Second World War, it wasn't just houses and schools that were being built. Churches and other places of worship were springing up in towns and new suburbs around the country; John Sanders saw the potential and expanded into the manufacture of ecclesiastical metalware – collection plates, tabernacles, monstrances, ciboria, chalices, lecterns, candlesticks

BOX 26
JEWISH MINORA.
WEDDING CAKE VASE.
HALF TABERNACLE BALLS.
MASS BELL STEMS.
VOTIVE CANDLE SOCKETS - SARKS.
CARIS - LADLES + SPOONS.

MORESBY

and crosses. There was no religious discrimination as far as he was concerned, being just as likely to make a piece for a Catholic or Anglican church as he was for a synagogue.

In 1971, W. J. Sanders merged with a badge-making company, W. J. Amor, and part of the business involved making medals and medallions. Under the name Amor-Sanders Pty Ltd, it continued for 25 years, even after John Sanders' retirement in 1984, until Dennis de Muth took over, and the company again started trading as W. J. Sanders.

Photographs of the old workshops and original owner are on the walls of the Marrickville headquarters; a cabinet contains Dennis de Muth's growing collection of early W. J. Sanders' pieces – tea sets, tankards, candlesticks – which he picks up whenever he comes across them. His aim is to have a mini-museum to celebrate the works of the company.

It's not just the past that Dennis de Muth is concentrating on – move slightly further into the workshop and you'll come across a few Logie rejects. The simple television trophies look particularly plain against work from other longtime clients, which include Admiralty House, St Mary's Cathedral, the Great Synagogue – all places that have precious metal objects that need restoring and who, occasionally, commission new works.

Dennis de Muth brings out photographs of the ciborium, chalice and plate the company had recently made for the Pope for Sydney World Youth Day. Elaborate pieces in silver and gold, with complex designs featuring eucalyptus leaves, and gum blossom studded with diamonds. And then he shows us a small gold-plated trophy, hand-decorated with a galloping horse framed inside a garland of leaves – the work of a young Argentinian woman who now lives north of Newcastle and approached him recently about work as a chaser. Hand-chasing –'hammering on metal to make shapes', as Dennis de Muth describes it – is almost a dead art in this country. 'The last time anyone did it here was about 30 years ago – having her here adds another dimension to what we can do.' She's in Marrickville the day we visit to pick up more work; Dennis de Muth has bought her a set of the tools she needs for the job.

It's noticeable that, as well as workers who have been at it for decades, there are a few young men among the dozen or so employed at W. J. Sanders – one came through art school to concentrate on restoration; another is training in the manufacturing side.

Dennis de Muth says he pays them a decent amount – more than an apprentice's wages – as a way of encouraging them to stay. 'I want this business to be going in 100 years' time,' he says.

It's the sort of job, you discover when you talk to the workers, that you could stay in for life. Sparrow (who got his name as 'the littlest boy in the surf patrol') has been at it for 48 years, ever since he was a teenager. He worked for one of the other manufacturing silversmiths around in Sydney at the time, and learnt many of the skills involved in the trade. But it's spinning that fascinated him when he started, and spinning that he does now, in a section at the back of the workshop, at his bench with Bunsen burner in one corner, and flat circles of metal and chucks scattered on the benchtop. Leaning against the bench is a group of steel-ended rods with long, thick wooden handles, prehistorically dark and wearing the signs of decades' worth of effort – you can almost make out the weight of a human body behind them. Sparrow takes a circle of nickel silver, heats it over the Bunsen burner until it's red-hot, and attaches it to the lathe, alongside a chuck for a chalice bowl. With the lathe spinning at high speed and the steel end of the rod against the nickel silver, he leans his shoulder into the long wooden handle and within seconds the circle of metal, seemingly as soft and malleable as plasticine, forms over the bowl shape. 'I loved watching that as a kid – I still do.'

He picks the metal, hot more from friction now, from the chuck with an old fork. Nothing special, not a fork that W. J. Sanders would have made – his handmade tongs have been mislaid for a moment – and dunks the embryonic bowl into a bucket of cold water before he starts spinning it again and again, carefully shaping it until the ever-thinning metal reaches the top of the chuck. He gets pleasure, he says, out of spinning 'the big horse trophies, but they don't have so many of them now – crystal is great, but it can break'.

Hanging on the wall near his workbench are hundreds of thin metal templates of varying sizes for crosses, ribbons and scrolls, boomerangs, all grouped together – used to decorate trophies and other silverware. On shelving on the other side, chucks of various shapes and sizes are piled up – when people bring their silverware with pieces missing, they can ferret through the chucks to look for likely matches.

Upstairs a couple of men are polishing metalware, using lathe-like machines with tiny black mops attached, spinning at high speed. One's working on a silver salver, the other on a strange metal object like a whisky flask. No one wants to say what it is. Eventually it comes out that it's a contraceptive device from the 1840s. I don't ask how it works. W. J. Sanders restores a lot of old medical equipment – collectibles, I am told, among doctors.

Polishing is one of the more meticulous jobs in the place – polish too much and engraving and hallmark can disappear forever, the manufacturing silversmith equivalent of dropping a Ming vase.

Back downstairs, a worker is sitting at a bench assessing battered and blackened pieces of silver for repair. He's estimating how many hours will be needed to take each apart, clean and polish it, make new pieces, and put it back together again. 'It's not for me to say whether it's worth it or not,' he says, picking up a Britannia silver teapot. 'It could have great sentimental value.' There are two schools of thought to restoration, says Dennis de Muth. 'One is to leave it, the other is to restore. If you don't do anything, the piece will break down eventually. We restore in a way that in five or 10 years' time you wouldn't know it had been touched.'

At another workbench, manufacturing silversmith Matthew Mulligan is filing back segments from a light – segments the size of dangling earrings, hexagonal in shape with a star in the middle. A few weeks earlier he'd been working on the holy vessels used by the Pope. He's been working for the company for 22 years, ever since he moved away from making medical cabinets and other scientific equipment. Another recent job was working on a holy vessel to hold the Torah – a piece that had been ordered to honour the owner's parents. 'I've seen many wondrous things here,' says Matthew Mulligan. 'I've made many wondrous things.'

Haystacks

Terrence Carroll wants to show us his devil's stick. It's in the back of his truck, and is never too far away from him. It stands almost as tall as he does, of bleached timber, could be some sort of gum, with a few cracks in it, three slender metal tines on the end. He's had it for 20 or 25 years, he reckons; he can't quite remember how long. Once a bloke's got a devil's stick, he doesn't let go of it, he says. He can keep the same one all his life if he's careful; he gets used to handling it, to the way it fits his body. He holds his pitchfork up to his eye, like a gun, and then passes it over for me to do the same. There's a slight bow to it – the handle isn't as straight as it looks head-on. You want to find one that's right for the way you pitch – left or right – get the wrong one 'and you'll get blisters on blisters. A devil's stick can make or break a man.'

For 30-odd years, Terrence Carroll used the pitchfork when he was making haystacks around Ganmain, a town of 650, between Wagga Wagga and Narrandera. The town describes itself on the name sign as you drive in as the 'sheaf hay centre'. Until a few years ago, there would be haystacks, some as tall as three-storey buildings, in paddocks all around the area – maybe 100 haystacks in a good year, sometimes a few to a paddock, looking like old-fashioned loaves of bread, plump with rounded ends and overhanging eaves, no two exactly alike. If you knew what you were looking at, says Terrence Carroll, you could tell who'd built which haystack. One stack builder went for steeper rooves, another's had almost no rooves at all, the ends of another's was rounder, and one man's, 'I wouldn't like to say, but his haystacks weren't as neat as some.' The area was settled by Victorians, he says, and most probably the design of haystacks was brought up from there. In South Australia, the German settlers built square haystacks with square corners.

Nowadays, open-sided sheds in paddocks around Ganmain hold big round bales of hay, machine cut, rolled and tied, uniform in size and lacking in character. They're easier and quicker to make, 'but you miss seeing the haystacks, you certainly do, but you don't miss building them, the physical work'.

Building haystacks is a skill passed down through families, from grandfather to father, from father to son. Several generations of Terrence Carroll's family built haystacks and it was something he expected to pass down to his sons, and for his grandsons, in time, to learn. That didn't happen – the knowledge ended, in his family, with him. His sons 'handled the hay' around the farm when they were younger, but never got around to learning how to make haystacks. Not that he'd necessarily want them to do it, it's such hard work. He's kicking himself that he doesn't have many photos of haystack building – he brings out the few snaps he does have – but it was work, something he'd known all his life, and as much part of the seasons as harvesting.

Several years ago, Terrence Carroll and a few other local haystack makers went to Werribee Zoo in Victoria for two weeks, taking 1500 sheaves of hay with them. They were there to put thatched rooves on some African-style huts. 'We thought we were putting a bit of straw on a couple of animal shelters, but it was more than that.'

There's still the odd haystack maker in the district, but the trade has essentially died out. There are a few reasons for that, says Ganmain chaff merchant Barrie Logan. Manpower is the biggest thing – if you had the choice, you'd find something else to do in the middle of summer 'and occupational health and safety don't help. You'd have to have a skyhook to be up that high off the ground, you're supposed to have a safety harness. How you'd rig up a safety harness in the middle of a haystack in the middle of a paddock, I don't know.'

Barrie Logan and Terrence Carroll never heard of anyone falling off a haystack. 'Hay's very slippery,' says Terrence Carroll. 'If you have a tight finish to the sheaf, and the hay's good quality it's like stacking cakes of soap.' If you came off a haystack, he says, 'you'd know it...or you mightn't know it, specially right off the top.'

It's not just the haystacks that would be a problem with the authorities. First step in the stack-building process is to make sheaves from the oat and wheat grown for the purpose (different from that grown for grain, and one that stays sweeter in the hay). 'They stopped making the machine to cut the hay in about 1950,' says Barrie Logan. 'It didn't have a lot of guards on it – you would've had to rebuild it to make it up to the safety standards they'd want now. You could keep using them as long as you never had an accident, same as the haystacks. You could keep building them as long as you never fell off them. If you did, they'd come out and you'd probably lose your farm.'

In the traditional way, hay is cut early in the season, before the heat of the summer and before the grain matures. Full grain, says Terrence Carroll, 'blows up a horse's joints, puts them off their diet'. Armful-sized amounts of hay are tied into sheaves, tightly enough to cope with being handled several times during the stack-making process. A gang of workers goes around the paddock and stands the sheaves up into stooks, tepee-shaped groups of about 15 sheaves. These are left out in the elements for at least three weeks to cure. It doesn't matter if it rains, says Barrie Logan. 'Water will run off a well-made stook.' It's more of a problem now with the round bales, he says, the hay being cut and left to dry on the ground before being rolled.

Haystack building happens in unshaded paddocks, with the bleached hay reflecting the sun's heat, through the hottest part of the year – from the end of November and stretching into March. Terrence Carroll wore a thermometer around his neck one year; when it got to 50 degrees Celsius, he took it off. 'I didn't want to know.'

Gangs of seven – four in the paddock and three on the stack – would regroup from year to year. 'They'd turn up every year at the same time, they'd like it,' says Barrie Logan. 'It was very hard work but in those days, people thrived on that.' They were local farmers, like Terrence Carroll, or men in search of casual work, or those on the seasonal work circuit. 'At one stage, cowboys from Queensland used to come down every year,' says Barrie Logan. 'Some of the top rodeo riders – they used to follow the rodeo circuit down here, work all week and go off at the weekend.'

Work would start with some gangs by seven in the morning, others by six-thirty, with half-hour smokos in the morning and afternoon and 'an hour off for dinner' in the middle of the day. 'We'd work until close to six,' says Terrence Carroll. 'You're looking for a beer when you're finished.'

It takes 'two and a bit days' to build an 90-tonne haystack as tall as a three-storey building, starting with the basic shape marked out on the ground in the middle of a paddock. 'Four blokes, what you'd call paddock men', says Terrence Carroll, would shift the sheaves from the stooks onto lorries or horse-drawn carts. Horses, he says, could get around a field better than a truck – they were more careful, and didn't overheat or run out of fuel. As the stack got higher, a motorised elevator would be used to move the sheaves from the lorry. Blokes would use the elevator, too, to get up and down the stack – something else for occupational health and safety to worry about. 'Sheaf turners', working incredibly quickly, would be on the stack, ready to hand the sheaves over to the haystack builders.

There are several parts to a sheaf, says Terrence Carroll, who worked as a sheaf turner with his brother for a few summers, and it makes a stack builder's job easier if the sheaf is handed to him the right way. 'Depending on where he is in the stack, you'd know whether it's knots up or knots down, butts out, heads out. He didn't want to be picking a sheaf up and twisting it around.' Knots up one row, he says, and knots down the next so it fits tightly. Jump up and down on a haystack, says Barrie Logan, and 'it's like an innerspring mattress'.

A rhythm would be set up as the gang worked, the stack builder going strictly by eye and feel. 'No measures, no gauges, no spirit levels, nothing to go by,' says Terrence Carroll. 'You see a 90-tonne haystack that's well built, it's a work of art, that's for sure. You've got to keep it pretty level because you get a stack that's not, and it'll slip out on you.' That happened to him once. 'The whole end just went, 20 tonne down on the ground. It happened that quick, I was up the top and all of a sudden, I was down. I lost a bit of skin, but didn't get buried under the hay or anything.'

The blokes would tell yarns or play practical jokes, 'putting grease on your pitchfork or a snake in your tuckerbox', or listen to the wireless – 'test cricket if it was on. You had to put up with the heat, there was no way out of it – you had to find ways to take your mind off it. Anything to fill the day.' In more recent years, young blokes 'would have the wireless on FM, pop music, full bore. You couldn't have a conversation because the music was too loud.'

A haystack can last for seven or eight years in a paddock. It might get discoloured with the weather, but the walls will be as solid as weatherboard, and virtually mouse-proof. Most of the time the haystacks weren't up for more than a year – they'd be dismantled as needed, and sent to the chaff cutter. At its peak, Ganmain had three or four chaff cutters in town; now there's just Logan & Hitchens, housed in tin sheds, with rough tree-trunk posts holding up the patched sheets of corrugated iron. In a good year, about 10,000 tonnes of hay from the district is processed through Logan & Hitchens; it's been less in the past few years because of the drought.

Sheaf hay goes through the cutters better than the round bales, says Terrence Carroll. Often the bale hay has to be put through twice to make the chaff fine enough. 'The horse'll sort out what he wants and what he doesn't,' he says. 'Too many longer straws, and they're left in the bottom of the feed box.'

The machinery at Logan & Hitchens looks as if it's been there for a century. Just before the hay heads into the cutter it goes through a plume of steam to soften it. It comes out the other end warm and slippery, speckled green, and straight into a bag printed with Ganmain Prime Wheaten Chaff Packed by Logan & Hitchens. 'Cut it on the green side and it tastes better and looks better in the bag,' says Terrence Carroll. 'You buy your fruit and vegies on look, chaff buyers do the same. They like the colour.' Racetracks, top racehorse trainers and pony clubs in New South Wales and Queensland have been buying chaff from Logan & Hitchens for years; it's still good stuff but some local farmers would tell you chaff from haystacks is better.

Back in Barrie Logan's office, he has a calendar on his wall, showing haystack building in the old days. He pulls out an old calendar from a desk drawer with another old photo on it, of a horse-drawn cart and men with pitchforks. At Terrence Carroll's farm, there's a 2009 calendar on the kitchen wall from Riverina Machinery with a photo of round bales, industrial in size, stacked up on a truck in a paddock. 'They're not nearly as pretty as the haystacks,' he says.

Haystacks

HORN

Acknowledgements

I could not have written this book without help from a number of people. I would like to thank my family for their support, and friends and colleagues who, between them, have given me ideas, encouragement and accommodation. In particular, Gina Shrubsall, Edwina Corlette, Wendy Howitt, Hossein and Angela Valamanesh, Paul Greenaway, Michael Fitzgerald, Sean Morris, Gaye Murray, Louise Pfanner, Ed Woodley, Paul Gordon-Smith, Andy from Fyxomatosis, the staff of Parkers Sydney Fine Art Supplies, and, above all, UM.

I had no intention of writing a book before Diana Hill and Kay Scarlett of Murdoch Books suggested it, so many thanks to them for thinking I had it in me, and for being supportive all the way. Thanks, too, to Katrina O'Brien for her careful handling of the project. And, of course, I'd especially like to thank Hugh Ford, both for his inspired design, which surpassed all my expectations, and for being such a pleasure to work with.

Max Dupain once said 'All industry has an aesthetic and it is up to the photographer to discover it.' Oliver Strewe found beauty in places no one else would have; he needs a special mention, too, for his ideas, and enthusiasm towards the project.

More than anything, though, I'm extremely grateful to all the people featured in the book for being trusting enough to let us through the doors in the first place (and thanks, too, to the one who wouldn't) and, once we were in, for being so generous with their time and knowledge. Without them, there would be no book.

Published in 2010 by Pier 9, an imprint of Murdoch Books Pty Limited

Murdoch Books Australia
Pier 8/9
23 Hickson Road
Millers Point NSW 2000
Phone: +61 (0) 2 8220 2000
Fax: +61 (0) 2 8220 2558
www.murdochbooks.com.au

Murdoch Books UK Limited
Erico House, 6th Floor
93–99 Upper Richmond Road
Putney, London SW15 2TG
Phone: +44 (0) 20 8785 5995
Fax: +44 (0) 20 8785 5985
www.murdochbooks.co.uk

Publisher: Diana Hill
Photographer: Oliver Strewe
Designer: Hugh Ford
Project Editor: Katrina O'Brien
Production: Kita George

Part of the Elfin Cars chapter first appeared in *The Australian's* 'Wish' magazine in October 2005.

National Library of Australia Cataloguing-in-Publication Data

Author: Keens, Leta.
Title: Shoes for the Moscow Circus: Scenes from a hidden world. From foundries and flagmakers to stonemasons and taxidermists / Leta Keens; photographer Oliver Strewe.
ISBN: 9781741964677 (hbk.)
Other Authors/Contributors:
Strewe, Oliver, 1950-
Dewey Number: 338.6420994

A catalogue record for this book is available from the British Library.

PRINTED IN CHINA

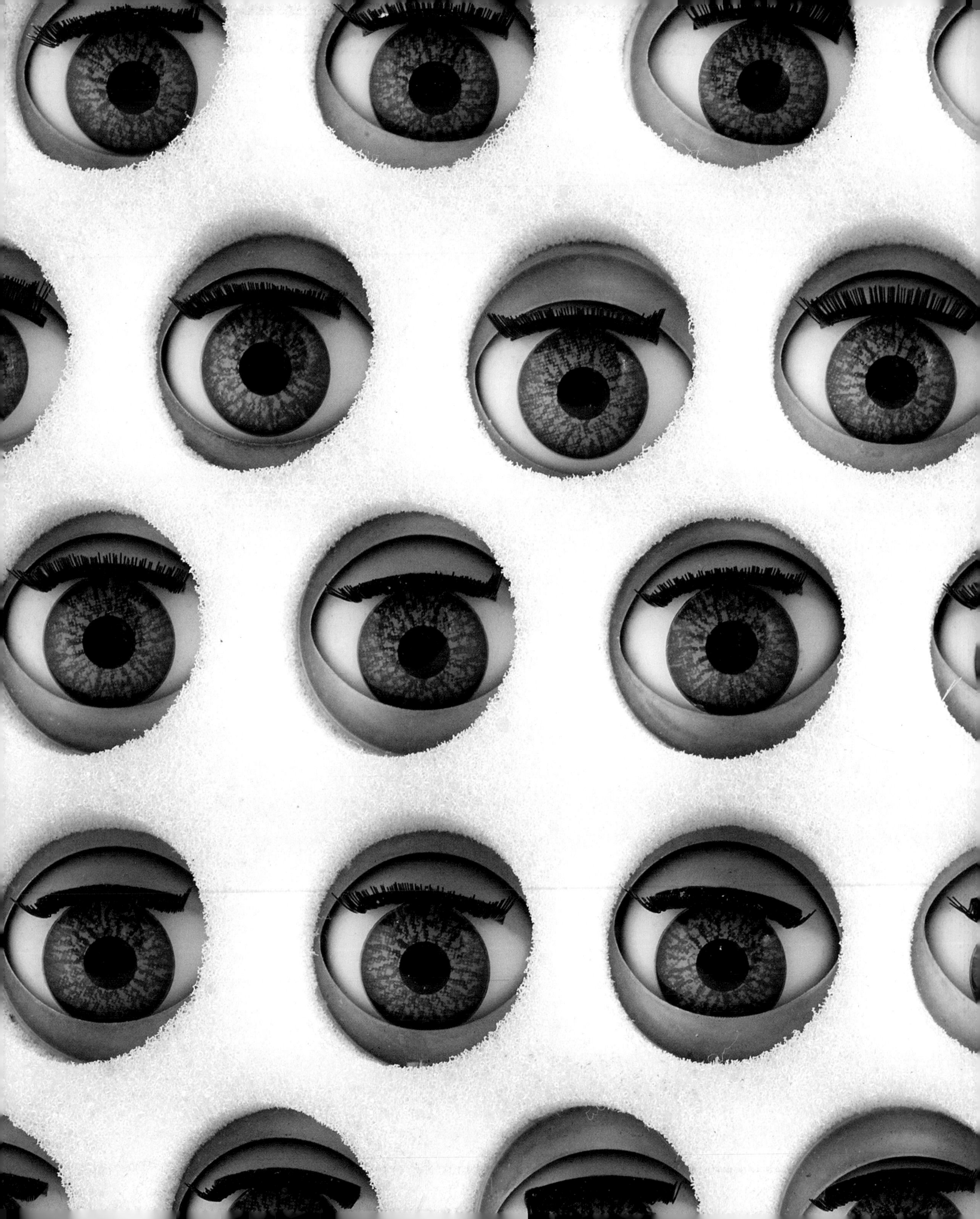